Jewish Humor Stories For Kids

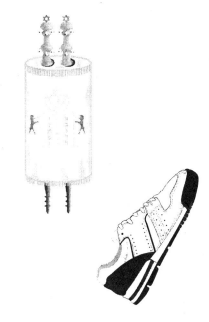

PITS**POP**ANY

NEW YORK ◆ JERUSALEM

PRINTING HISTORY:

First Printing - August, 1998
Second Printing - February, 2000

Published by Pitspopany Press
Copyright © 1998

PITSPOPANY PRESS books may be purchased for
educational or special sales by contacting:

Marketing Director, Pitspopany Press
40 East 78th Street, Suite 16D
New York, New York 10021
Fax: (212) 472-6253
E-mail: pop@netvision.net.il
Web: www.pitspopany.com

ISBN: 0-943706-77-7 — Cloth
ISBN: 0-943706-78-5 — Softcover

Printed in Hungary

The Judaica Librarians' Choice Award

In November of 1997, I assumed an interesting position with the Association of Jewish Libraries: I would chair a short story competition to encourage unpublished authors to submit stories of Jewish content for grades four through eight. The first year, the stories were to contain wit, cheer, or even a disposition toward the absurd. In short, they were to be humorous.

The idea for this book belongs to Yaacov Peterseil, who recognized the need for Jewish short stories in English, for this age group. There have been very few collections of original short stories published since the *World Over Storybooks* came off the press, over forty years ago. Today, the stories of K'Tonton are being taken out of Sadie Rose Weilerstein's original book and published as single picture books.

The decades of the seventies and eighties and into the nineties have been the decades of Jewish folklore, featuring stories from the Talmud, and from collections gathered and preserved in Israel at the International Folklore Archives by Dov Noy and others. They have added immeasurably to the wealth of material available for Jewish students. But they have not featured the contemporary scene.

The object of this first collection is to do just that: to present the Jewish student with entertaining works that are both believable and modern, featuring Jewish families living in the world, today.

The group of stories submitted to the five impartial judges, all experienced Hebrew day school librarians, came from around the globe. There were stories from the United States and Canada, and several from Israel. Over 150 people asked for the competition's rules. Of those selected as winner and runners-up, two were from the United States and two from Israel. The winning story was by a psychologist from Michigan.

It has been a pleasure to represent the Association of Jewish Libraries and to participate in the AJL-Pitspopany Press *Librarians' Choice Award* competition.

Hazel Karp, Past President AJL   Atlanta, GA

ALSO AVAILABLE IN THIS SERIES:

Jewish Mystery Stories For Kids
Jewish Sci-Fi Stories For Kids

Table of Contents

Jewish
Humor Stories
For Kids

Breakfast
Without
Bagels

Harold I. Mathis *is a licensed clinical psychologist and marriage counselor. He has a private practice in West Bloomfield, Michigan, a suburb of Detroit. He is married and has two children.*

Harold has a keen sense of humor. While this story is not autobiographical, it is in many ways a psychological study of a segment of Jewish middle America. It is filled with real people and events that ring true.

As far as the ending...well, that's a bagel of a different flavor!

*W*hatever Harvey asks for, Harvey gets.

Don't misunderstand. Harvey doesn't ask for a lot, and he doesn't ask often. He fools you that way.

Everyone thinks he's unselfish, prudent, and cost-conscious, but, they're wrong.

Harvey is a saver.

He saves comic books. He saves Israeli postage stamps. And he saves Detroit Red Wings trading cards.

Harvey also saves up what he asks for. He doesn't ask for lots of small stuff, but that's not because he's thrifty. That's because he's saving up for a "Big Request."

But this time Little Harvey has gone too far. He's just plain asking for too much.

My name is Jeff Kinder. I'm 16. Harvey is my 11-year-old brother. For nearly a year, our family has been living in the remote farm community of Hillside Township. To locate Hillside, you will need a map of Michigan. Unfold the map. Right off, you will see that Michigan's lower peninsula is shaped like the large padded mitten your mom uses to pull hot Pyrex pans out of the oven. Now, hold up your own right hand and look at your palm. Notice, in the center of your hand, just below the fingers is a plump little hill. Hillside is on the left side of that hill.

If you're coming to Hillside, don't expect Detroit or even Lansing. Our downtown is just a few squat buildings north of the railroad tracks on Route M-61. Unless you're held up by a train, you'll breeze right by. Fortunately, freight trains a hundred boxcars long, roll through the center of town every twenty minutes or so, backing up traffic for five miles in both directions. Otherwise, you'd miss us for sure.

Don't get the wrong impression. We may rely on well water and septic tanks, but Hillside is no backwater hicktown. We have a Starbuck's Cafe with a 24-hour ATM machine, a rock 'n roll radio station, an elementary school and enough houses of worship to accommodate seven religious denominations, none of them Jewish.

As far as that goes, you won't find a synagogue or a temple in Hillside, Hilltop, or all of Uphill County, no matter how long and hard you look. But it would be a mistake to jump to the wrong conclusion. It's not that Jews are unwelcome around here.

Jews, like bagels, are just unknown around here. I'm sure we are the only Jewish family within a hundred miles, one hundred and fifty, if you count Saginaw Bay. Besides, we haven't told anyone around here that we are Jewish.

In spite of this, my spoiled younger brother is determined to have a Bar Mitzvah.

Where we live, in Hillside, the population isn't dense enough to qualify us for our own high school, so I attend Hilltop High. The City of Hilltop is much larger and much more commercial than Hillside. Hill-top has an indoor shopping mall, three gas stations, a Kinko's, and a bowling alley with two regulation-size lanes. Kids from all the surrounding communities who feel like going to high school (and most of them don't), attend Hilltop High.

If you succeeded in finding the town of Hillside on your hand, you should be able to guess where the City of Hilltop is.

In case you're curious, or even if you're not, I'll explain why, almost a year ago, the Kinder family moved from our very urban, very Jewish neighbor-hood in Southfield, to this totally gentile, rural outpost in the palm of Michigan farm country.

In the process, I will also explain how it hap-pened that my very Jewish Dad got appointed to be the official Hillside town Santa Claus.

The present problem, though, is my micro-brained brother, Harvey, who insists upon having a Bar Mitzvah. In Southfield, that would be fine. No problem. That's where I had my Bar Mitzvah. But here in Hillside, a Bar Mitzvah would totally blow our cover and ruin everything. Besides, can you imag-ine anything weirder than the son of Santa having a Bar Mitzvah?

It's mainly because I had a super Bar Mitzvah that Harv wants one, too. When the kid's not com-peting with me, he's copy-catting me. For example, take the time back when we were living in Southfield, when the two of us decided to spend our Hanukkah gelt at Kessler's Men's Wear on Nine Mile Road. The store was called "Men's Wear," but they mostly sold clothing for boys.

My pal Solly's granddad owned Kessler's Men's Wear. Solly Kessler was my best friend. Solly was in my Hebrew school class and later attended my Bar Mitzvah.

Solly was a good guy, but I couldn't stand his grandfather, his *zaydie*. The old man was very annoying. From the moment Harvey and I walked into his store, Kessler followed around behind us to make sure that we didn't steal anything. He acted as if we might pull a shoelace out of a sneaker and pocket it. In my whole life, I've never even swiped a packet of sweetener from the lunchroom, yet Old Man Kessler treated me like I was a convicted kleptomaniac out on parole from a juvenile detention center.

His favorite facial expression was a scowl. If Kessler ever smiled, he did it behind closed doors, in the privacy of his own home where he wouldn't get caught. His accent was so thick that not only couldn't I understand him, I could hardly tell he was speaking English.

Anyway, on this particular occasion it was still only Spring, but I was already dreaming of summer camp. My parents promised to send me to Camp

Moshava in Michigan's Irish Hills. It was with camp on my mind that I decided to buy myself a pair of bright red swimming trunks. So, naturally, Harvey had to have a pair, too.

At the time, I was twelve, but Harv was only seven, and he wasn't even scheduled to go to summer camp.

Regardless, he insisted on buying the exact same swimming trunks. Of course, we were nowhere near the same size, so his didn't fit. Even in the store, he had to hold them up with both hands to remain decent. Naturally, when we got home, Mom wasn't happy.

The next day, Mom went back to the store and asked Mr. Kessler if she could return Harvey's swimsuit, but Solly's grandpa said store policy didn't permit returns on bathing suits.

Mom asked him, "Who sets store policy?"

Mr. Kessler said, "I do."

Mom tried her darndest to get him to change his mind, but Old Man Kessler wouldn't budge. He refused to take the trunks back or even to exchange them for a smaller size.

I was burning mad, but Mom was quite calm.

"You have to understand," she told me later.

"What do you mean?" I asked. "A seven-year-old kid buys the wrong size bathing suit, and Old Man Kessler won't take it back! That's not right!"

"No, it is not right," Mom agreed. "But you have to understand Jake Kessler."

"What's there to understand? The guy's a jerk!"

"Jake Kessler is a survivor of 'The Camps.'"

Suddenly, I understood. I knew what Mom meant. I had seen the numbers tattooed on Kessler's arm. Mom was telling me that Old Man Kessler wasn't mean. He was tough. Only the tough survived the Holocaust. And even among the toughest, most had perished. Maybe Old Man Kessler should have taken the swimsuit back, but it was really because of Harvey's copy-catting that I ended up with two identical pairs of red swimming trunks.

Even if Harvey weren't a copycat, I could understand why he might have been jealous of my Bar Mitzvah. My Bar Mitzvah was a blast. I know that I made a few mistakes chanting my Haftorah, but no one seemed to care, except Rabbi Mintz. I could tell Mintz was upset, by the way he kept clenching his tallit in his fist during my reading. But, even though it was true, I don't think he should have mentioned that I skipped a page.

However, I hope everyone remembers that I was the one who wanted to have two parties, one for the adults and one for my friends. I told my parents that combining the two groups would create an explosive blend — like mixing fertilizer with diesel fuel. I warned them, but they didn't listen. They vetoed my proposal. Nevertheless, guess who was blamed for the tumult, the rumpus and all the broken glass?

You guessed it: The Bar Mitzvah boy!

What did they expect when a bunch of rowdy, unsupervised teens have access to a free bar? Sure, I gave permission. But what kind of bartender obeys a thirteen-year-old kid?

And I admit that I passed out the water pistols, but I never imagined mature adults would get so upset over a little bit of moisture. He denies it, but I still suspect it was Harvey who called the police.

Harvey and I are brothers, but the only thing we have in common is our wiry hair. I'm tall and thin like my Uncle Bernie. Harvey is just like my Dad, perpetually on a strict diet that he rigorously adheres to, if you don't count his insatiable appetite for bagels.

Like my dad, Harvey always tells the bagel man, "Scoop out the bagel, and remember, no cream cheese." Of course, like my dad, he puts plenty of jam on the bagel, and always washes it down with a danish.

Harvey calls himself stocky. But we all know he's fat.

Way back, when Mom first brought Baby Harvey home from the hospital, we were living in a big colonial house in the wealthy suburb of Bloomfield, Michigan. I was only five, but that was a day I will always remember.

Before Harv came along, I was the king, an only child. No matter what anybody tells you, and grown-ups do lie, in America, absolutely nothing beats the supreme luxury of being an only child. If I pouted, our whole family did somersaults trying to make me smile, which, to this day, Dad blames for his bad back.

Then along came Infant Harvey. What an ugly wrinkled baby! Not at all like the magazine pictures of the Ivory Soap Baby they showed me and told me he would look like. In a way, I was glad he was so ghastly. How could they prefer that ugly monster to me? Wasn't I their, "cutesy little Jeffypoo?"

Boy, was I mistaken! All of a sudden Baby Harv was getting all the royal attention, and Mom was shipping me off to a public institution called kindergarten.

It wasn't just Mom. Dad did an about-face, too.

Before Harvey came into our lives, Dad's main purpose in life was amusing me. He was constantly serenading me with silly songs and acting *meshugah* — that means nutty. Dad loved to clown around. Anything to make me laugh. He actually practiced before a mirror, twisting his face into a gnarly knot just so I would giggle.

After Harvey was born, the circus left town. During the whole next year, Dad-the-Clown became Dad-the-Grouch. Mom said Dad was in a state of depression because he'd lost his job, but I blamed the downshift in Dad's personality on Harvey.

Now, when I think back on it, Mom could have been right, because it wasn't long after Harvey was born that the four of us moved into our grandmother's house in Southfield. Our parents didn't want to move to Bubbie's, but they had no choice. Dad being out of work, they couldn't meet their mortgage payment on our expensive house in Bloomfield.

I know that leaving our large home, to share Bubbie's cramped upstairs flat in Southfield, hurt Dad's pride. For two months, he seldom left the house, except to look for work. Dad had been proud of our Bloomfield colonial. Even though it wasn't his fault, he felt guilty and embarrassed about moving the family into his mother's place. Mom said Dad felt like a failure and was ashamed. According to Mom, that's when Dad really began to pile on the pounds.

Mom hated living with Dad's Mom. I don't remember much about the house in Bloomfield, but I do remember it was roomier and friendlier back there. No matter how loud I blasted the TV, no one complained. Also, the tables were higher than they were at Bubbie's house. In the Bloomfield house, I had to climb up the drawers to reach the top of Mom's dresser. At Bubbie's, we had less space, less noise, less freedom, and lower furniture.

One summer in Southfield, Harv made the acquaintance of a stray mongrel dog he found sniffing our garbage. I named our new pet Grundgy. Together, me, Harv and the neighborhood kids hosed Grundgy down, and bathed him in Harv's kiddie pool. All us kids loved Grundgy. Harv and I wanted to keep him, but we had to ask Bubbie's permission.

In fairness to Bubbie, it was the only time I remember her saying "no" to either of us. The next day Grundgy was gone. I don't know what happened to him. Maybe one of the other kids adopted him. I'd like to think so. In spite of my disappointment, I could understand Bubbie's decision. Bubbie and Zaydie were senior citizens. They had lived alone for many years. Even though Dad was their son, taking our large family into their small upstairs apartment could not have been easy. Grundgy would have been just too much.

As nice as she was to Harv and me, Bubbie didn't always seem to understand how difficult living there was for my parents. Mom especially missed having her own home. Everyone said the reason that Dad lost his job and Mom lost her house was because the company Dad worked for went bankrupt. But I blamed it on Harvey. To me, it was obvious. We were cruising along at 80 miles per hour down the Good Life highway, B.H. (Before Harvey was born). That was the obvious turning point. A.H. (After Harvey) the engine threw a rod, the clutch burned out, the tires went flat, and the transmission froze up tight. It was straightforward cause and effect.

For the next nine years, we lived with Bubbie and Zaydie.

It was a harder adjustment for my parents than for me, even though none of my friends were living with their grandparents. Just us. As a matter of financial necessity, our life-style became constricted. We rarely ate out or attended movies, and I could never go with my friends to rock concerts. We made do without cable TV, designer clothes, and costly toys such as electronic games. It took awhile but as we adjusted to our humbler circumstances, some of the pressure eased, and Dad's mood gradually improved, even though he changed jobs once or twice a year.

In our family, everything was discussed around the kitchen table. I say "discussed," but we had some pretty fierce arguments. Dad's employment was always a hot topic. Mom repeatedly insisted that her brother Bernie could get Dad a job as a quality-control inspector in the automobile plant where he worked. But this only made Dad angry. Dad hated Uncle Bernie, and angrily refused Mom's urging. I remember Dad's exact words, "I don't want no job from that crooked brother of yours, or anybody else. Any job I get, I'll get on my own, and that's that!"

21

Uncle Bernie was a union boss. I admired my Uncle Bernie, and thought he was daring and adventurous.

I only met Uncle Bernie twice. One time, he took me with him to walk the picket line. It was scary, but fun. We carried signs, booed the scabs and chanted slogans, while the police stood in riot gear protecting the strikebreakers. The second time, Mom couldn't get a sitter, so she took me with her to bail Uncle Bernie out of jail.

Mom called Dad stubborn for refusing to let Uncle Bernie help him. Harvey probably gets his stubbornness from Dad's side of the family.

It didn't help that Harv and I fought a lot. No matter how much I teased him, the kid still followed me around like the tail on a lizard. Whether Mom told me to look after him, which she often did, or whether he tagged along on his own, it seemed that everywhere I went, Harvey had to go, too. And I didn't like it.

When Harvey turned five, we were forced to share my bedroom, which only made matters worse. It was mostly my fault we didn't get along, but the little creep was always into my Legos and other good stuff. Nothing was safe from Baby Harv, and no matter what terrible crimes he committed, my parents always took his side.

When I accidentally set the curtains on fire, I

was grounded for a week. It was a careless, dumb mistake, and I accepted my punishment. Yet, when Harvey deliberately pulled on the lamp cord in the living room, causing the lamp to fall off the table and break, he received no punishment at all. Many stunts that Harvey pulled were dangerous and he could have seriously hurt himself, but it was me who got into trouble if I tied him up and locked him in the closet for his own safekeeping.

Crowded as it was at Bubbie's house, I liked living there. I was president of the Southfield United Synagogue Youth chapter, and had lots of friends. Besides, Bubbie and Zaydie treated me great. They bought me toys, and they never hollered at me. In many ways they were nicer to me than my parents. Whenever I helped Bubbie carry packages or fold the laundry, she always gave me a quarter. Zaydie was a great story teller. He knew more jokes and riddles than anybody. All the magic tricks I can do with pieces of string, a few coins, or match sticks, I learned from Zaydie. I felt right at home in Southfield, and I strongly resisted the idea of moving away. Mom, however, was eager to move.

I knew we were barely getting by, and the only solution was for Dad to get a better job. Sundays were dedicated to Operation Secure Employment, conducted with the rigor of a military campaign, modeled after Dad's brief stint as a Private first class in the Marine Corps.

The Sunday ritual began promptly at 7:45 a.m. with Room Inspection.

"Atten-hut! Sergeant Jeffrey Kinder reporting for duty, Sir!"

"Atten-hut! Corporal Harvey Kinder reporting for duty, Sir!"

Room Inspection included beds, closets, and visible surfaces. After that, we had to go through close-order personal inspection. That covered hair, teeth, fingernails, uniform of the day, and school-work review. We took Inspection seriously. Our weekly allowances were largely based on Personal Inspection, especially schoolwork review. Any demerits found during Inspection had to be corrected before Morning Report, which was held at General Kinder's Command Post in the dining room.

Harvey once asked Dad how he rose from the rank of Pfc. to General. In his most serious tone, Dad attributed his elevation in rank to outstanding achievements and heroic actions above and beyond the call of duty.

"Like what?" asked Harvey.

"Like the fall of the Soviet Union, and the Peace Treaty between Egypt and Israel," Dad said, without cracking a smile.

"You did that!" Harv exclaimed, impressed.

"Single-handedly!" Dad replied.

The amazing thing was: I think Harvey actually believed him. Harvey could never tell when Dad was kidding.

The Kinder Brigade was entirely Dad's idea. We had no say. We were conscripted, which means, pressed into service against our will. I knew the whole army thing was a game, but I understood and fully accepted the underlying importance of going along with our mission. Harvey, on the other hand, took all the military claptrap seriously. Our understandings and attitudes may have differed but, once formed, the Kinder Brigade worked as a team, and like good soldiers we took pride in our outfit.

I don't think our family was especially secretive, but certain subjects were deemed "family matters" and were not discussed with "outsiders." Our financial condition and Dad's employment were two such subjects. Neither did we tell our friends about our Sunday military rituals. Had we done so, I'm sure our friends would have called us crazy and counseled us to mutiny or go AWOL.

Sundays, General Kinder commandeered the dining room table to use as his Command Post. Following Inspection, we had Morning Report.

We reported promptly at 8:30 a.m. to the Command Post to receive our orders. They were always the same. We were sent out on patrol to gather intelligence information. Gathering intelligence information meant scouting the news racks and buying newspapers that might contain relevant job ads. Meanwhile, using the computer, Dad scoured the Internet for leads. When we returned from patrol, we placed our pile of newsprint on the table to the left of Gen. Kinder's Macintosh computer. To the right of the Mac, the General kept a note pad, his coffee mug, and his trusty "no cream cheese" bagel. Dad spent most of Sunday at the computer composing letters of application for sales jobs advertised in the Sunday paper, or posted on the Net. This task, like everything else Dad did, was very organized.

First, Dad canvassed the want ads, circling with a yellow marking pen any position that struck him as a possible opportunity. To these prospects he would send out his *Standard Letter of Inquiry.* In the afternoons he did something similar, the only difference being that the afternoon inquiries went out by e-mail via the World Wide Web. On weekdays, after work, Dad would review the mail for replies. He would rank them by number. Number 1's were No Answers. Number 2's were Rejections. And Number 3's were Not Worth Its. Remarking on the day's yield, he might say, "We got a whole bushel of No. 1's today," or "I got three No. 2's and one No. 3 today." Very rarely did Dad receive what he called a "Hot Lead." Most of these Hot Leads, upon scrutiny, cooled down pretty fast to No. 3's, Not Worth It. Every month or so, a

Hot Lead would result in an interview.

Dad was no fancypants. His typical mode of dress might charitably be called, "Comfortably Casual." But for employment interviews, Dad was clean-shaven, his shoes were shinier than Uncle Bernie's black Buick after a wash and wax, and his good blue pants were pressed razor sharp. If Dad got the interview, he usually got the job. Like any good salesman, Dad could sell himself.

But sometimes, Dad returned from his meeting with a downcast look on his face. Then we knew that the interview had gone poorly. He usually blamed it on his weight, or on anti-Semitism, or both. He would say, "I could tell when I walked into the room I wasn't what they were looking for. They don't hire people with my kind of nose." Or he would say, "They were looking for one of those slim jims." He never revealed his exact weight to anybody, but Dad must be close to 300 pounds.

When a Hot Lead did pan out, Dad would change jobs. Usually, the new job was only slightly better than the one he had just given up. At one point, Dad seriously considered moving the family to Israel to live on a kibbutz with Uncle Yoav and Aunt Tzippi. Aunt Tzippi is Mom's sister. Uncle Yoav is a *Sabra*, a native-born Israeli.

Every night, Dad and Uncle Yoav wrote back and forth by e-mail. Harv and I also enjoyed an e-mail correspondence with our Israeli cousins, Yael and Gershon, whom we never met.

Life on the kibbutz sounded just like Camp Moshava. Our cousins described their dorm and the fun they had eating in the big dining hall. On the kibbutz, they had cows, goats, chickens, dogs, cats, and even two parrots and a monkey. From Yael and Gershon's letters, it appeared their life consisted of hiking, playing sports, and going on outings. Harv was eager to move to the kibbutz. It sounded pretty good even to me.

My Aunt Tzippi and my Israeli cousins can read and write English, but Uncle Yoav only knows Hebrew. Aunt Tzippi is Yoav's e-mail interpreter. Dad says Hebrew is a strange language. If you don't put in the dots, it's difficult to read. If you do put in the dots, it's difficult to write. Dad is fluent in Hebrew, but our computer isn't. Our Mac can only e-mail in English.

Both Harv and I attended Hebrew School, and as I said, I performed my Bar Mitzvah. The only Hebrew words I remember are *shalom* and *todah,* which mean hello and thank you. Harv was and is a much better student than I ever was. He could read Hebrew better when he was eight years old than I could after my Bar Mitzvah. I always valued friends and sports more than school, whereas Harvey was G&T, all the way. That's Gifted & Talented.

Harv was, and still is, nerdy. I prefer to be cool. He will deny it, but I'll bet Harvey actually enjoys doing homework. But that's only because he's lousy at sports. The only way you could teach Harvey to play basketball would be to explain it in a book.

It's hard to believe that only a year ago, Harvey and I were sharing a bedroom in our grandparents house in Southfield. We would probably still be there if it weren't for that Unexpected Letter.

It was just after the Fourth of July that Dad got the letter from FarMich. I was a freshman at Southfield High at the time, Harv was at Lathrop Elementary School. I remember we were all sitting downstairs in the family room. It was Sunday, and Dad was circling ads and sorting through his mail. He'd read each letter to himself and call out it's number, "Number 2!..., Number 2!..., Number 3!...." Suddenly, he burst out laughing. "Listen to this Number 3!"

After he read the letter out loud, I said, "What's so funny?" To me, it sounded like a typical business letter.

"Well, first of all, it's from FarMich. That's obviously a contraction of Farm-Michigan. But do you know what *fermisht* means in Yiddish?"

"No, what?" I answered.

"It means, all screwed up!"

"That is funny," I said, not really thinking it was so funny. FarMich and fermisht didn't sound *exactly* the same.

"But it still could be a good job," Harvey said.

"It's ridiculous!" Dad said. "I'd have to be fermisht to take it."

But Mom said, "Don't be so quick. It could be an opportunity."

"What? Do you really want us to move two hundred miles up north into the wilderness? Can you imagine me selling tractors to farmers?"

"How much harder can selling farm machinery be than selling office supplies?" Mom asked.

"But I don't know the first thing about farm machinery," Dad protested.

"You're smart, you'll learn," Mom assured him.

At Mom's insistence, and against his own judgement, Dad reluctantly inquired further. To his surprise and dismay, each inquiry met with encouragement from the company.

Twice, he drove up to Hillside and met with Vander Olafsen, the top guy at FarMich. When Dad returned after the first interview, we all huddled around badgering him with questions.

"How did it go?"

"What was it like?"

"Tell us about the town!"

"Tell us about the school!"

"Tell us about the people!"

"What are the kids like?"

"Tell us about the weather!"

"Hold on, hold on. I'll tell you about everything. Hillside is on the side of a hill, so all the houses are slanted and the cows have longer legs on one side than on the other, depending upon which side of the hill they live on, just so they can stand up straight."

Harvey interrupts, "Do the dogs and cats have longer legs on one side, too?"

I tell Harv that Dad is kidding. This makes Harv angry and frustrated.

"Come on, Dad, stop kidding around. Really tell us!"

"Okay. For real. Hillside is very different than Southfield. For starters, it's a very small town. There's only one school. The high school is in the nearby city of Hilltop.

"It appears to be almost entirely White. I didn't see any Black people on the streets or anywhere."

"Are there any Jewish families in Hillside?" asked Mom.

"I very much doubt it. Mr. Olafsen has a picture of Jesus on the wall of his office. Later, when I tried to find a bagel store in town, people asked me, 'What's a bagel?' What's a town without a bagel store!"

"None at all?"

"Not one of the stores I went into had even *heard* of bagels.

"I must have made a good impression, because

31

Mr. Olafsen offered me a very high salary, plus commission. He also offered to pay for our moving costs and I would receive a month of paid training. Of course, that's only if I survive the second interview."

Dad must have really booted their hard drive! We couldn't believe the salary and commission they were offering him. Combined, it came to twice what he had been making.

Another plus was the very low cost of living in Hillside compared to Southfield. Dad got a haircut in Hillside for a dollar and seventy-five cents that would have cost over three dollars in Southfield. And he didn't even have to make an appointment. He just walked in off the street.

Like any Jewish family, each of us had a different opinion. Mom was adamant that, if offered, Dad should take the job. In two years, she argued, we would be debt-free, and even have some savings. I knew the real reason Mom wanted to move was because she was so desperate to get out of Bubbie's house, where she felt like an imposing guest. Mom would have willingly moved us all to the South Pole, if it meant having her own igloo.

"At the end of two years," she declared, "if we decide Hillside is not for us, no matter where we go, it will be to a home of our own."

I definitely did not want to move. I had recently had my Bar Mitzvah and all my Southfield friends

32

would soon be having theirs. If we moved two hundred miles away, I would miss all the parties. I could see Dad was nervous. He protested that he had never been on a farm in his life, and couldn't tell a cow from a horse, unless he really got up close.

"How will a city slicker like me, who is firmly convinced that milk originates in a carton, sell farm equipment?" he asked. "Besides, I need my morning bagel to survive!"

Harvey persisted in arguing we should emigrate to Israel, and made a pest of himself skipping around the house singing Hava Nagillah.

At several points during our family discussions, the arguments became quite heated. I was the most obstinate and unruly. I protested, I cried, I pouted, I begged, I pleaded, I stamped my feet, I banged everything I could bang: doors, drawers, the phone, my hockey stick. But it didn't work.

Mom got her way. She forced Dad to consider the position. Once again, we really didn't have much choice about moving. Bubbie's house in Southfield was just too small for the six of us. For too long Dad had worked ten-hour days, Mom supplementing his income by providing daycare for the neighborhood kids. Even more than the money, our family needed a place of our own.

Dad agreed to go for the second interview. The interview took place during the heat of August. Sitting across from Mr. Olafsen, and the picture of Jesus, Dad was sweating. But from the way Dad explained it, it soon became apparent that Mr. O. was thinking far ahead, to winter.

Dad was totally unprepared for Vander Olafsen's strange proposal. Mr. O. made it seem like an afterthought, but Dad was later convinced that his new boss had decided what he was going to ask as soon as he laid eyes on Dad's ample belly. It turned out that Vander Olafsen needed a Santa Claus.

As he explained it, for years, as Hillside's largest employer and community leader, Mr. O. felt it was his civic duty to play the part of Santa at company and civic functions. He said that he absolutely dreaded being Santa and assumed the role reluctantly mainly because he had no gracious way of bowing out.

Until he met Dad, that is.

Mr. O. realized that Dad was so physically suited for the part, the town couldn't help but forgive him for understandably yielding the role to the candidate who best looked the part.

Mr. O. didn't present his Santa request as a condition of employment, which would probably have been illegal, but rather as a favor to himself. He was very smooth. Speaking informally, Vander Olafsen asked if, as a personal favor, Dad would mind spending a few days playing Santa. Mr. O. would pay him for his time, of course. Even though Vander didn't say so, to Dad it was transparently clear that getting the job depended on his willingness to play Santa.

You might suppose that this new wrinkle would have generated a whole new upheaval within our argumentative family, but you'd be wrong. Sounding like a chorus of high school cheerleaders, Mom and Harvey urged Dad to "do it, do it, do it." I was the lone dissenter, but that was only because I didn't want to leave Southfield. Dad looked the part, and with his sense of humor he seemed a natural. Finally, we all seemed very satisfied with the arrangement when, leave it to Harvey, the troublemaker, to bring up the issue of sacrilege.

Harvey had second thoughts. He went into a long impassioned speech about the many Jewish martyrs, like Rabbi Akiva, who, in every century, suffered and often gave up their lives defending their faith. He asked, "Wouldn't playing Santa do dishonor to their memory?" Harvey had hit a nerve. We were all very proud of our Jewish heritage and traditions.

Harvey pressed his point: "Isn't playing Santa a form of sacrilege?" he argued. "If asked by mean King Antiochus, do you think Yehuda HaMacabee would have marched around Tel Aviv in a Santa Claus suit?"

I wondered, how does that kid remember all that Hebrew school stuff? I don't.

I could see that Harvey's questions pleased Dad, who was not at all happy to have been selected to play Santa on the basis of his weight. But Mom was not pleased. She jumped into the debate with both feet.

First of all, she declared, Mr. Olafsen is not Antiochus. Second of all, Hillside is not Tel Aviv, which, by the way, didn't even exist back then. Third of all, Dad is not Judah the Macabee, and most important, role-playing Santa is not idolatry because Santa Claus is not a "false god," but a legendary figure, like Batman. Mom convinced Harvey that impersonating a make-believe character was not a form of worship. So Dad wouldn't be showing any disloyalty to Judaism by play-acting Santa or anybody else.

Personally, I don't think Harvey really cared, he just liked to argue. The kid's destined to become a lawyer. Dad labeled Mom's arguments "expedient rationalizations," but stopped objecting. We were surprised when even Uncle Yoav in Israel urged Dad, via e-mail, to take the job. Rather than being offended, as we assumed, Yoav found the notion of Dad playing Santa amusing. He pointed out that Dad would be doing a favor for the gentiles, just as non-Jews sometimes perform duties for us on Shabbat that are forbidden to Jews.

One part of our plan we kept secret from Uncle Yoav, because we knew, if told, he would be very upset. We collectively decided that it would be better, at least temporarily, not to advertise our religion to our new Hillside neighbors.

We weren't sure how Dad's new employer, with the picture of Jesus on the wall of his office, would take to hiring a Jew, especially a Jewish Santa Claus. Mom theorized that it might be a lot easier selling tractors to pig farmers if religion wasn't an issue. So, our religion was labeled a "family matter," not to be mentioned to "outsiders."

Mom said that concealing our faith wasn't secrecy, it was discretion. Discretion wasn't deception, it was just practical good sense. Dad hadn't had steady work in a long time. This was a good-paying position. We wanted to do everything possible to help Dad succeed and to avoid revealing anything that might jeopardize our sudden good fortune.

Dad tried to put a funny slant on things: "We are all in the same boat. Why make waves? Why rock the boat? Why put rocks in the boat? It's never a good idea to stand up in the boat. Especially not for an overweight Santa."

Another unanticipated change resulted from Dad's interviews with Vander Olafsen. Our family acquired a whole new name. Our last name was and still is Kinder, and that's the way dad wrote it on his application form. But, how was Mr. O. to know that we always pronounced Kinder so that it sounds like the "kinder" in kindergarten.

During the initial interview, Mr. Olafsen repeatedly mispronounced Kinder so that it rhymed with finder. At the time, and ever since, Dad has been too intimidated by Mr. Olafsen to correct the man. The error turned out to be prophetic. With Dad's new job, in more ways than one, we not only became richer, but kinder.

Those interviews took place about ten months ago. During our first month up north, while Dad was in training, and Harv and I attended school, we lived in two adjacent one-room cabins at the Hillside Motel. Mom spent her days accompanied by Mrs. Breen, the real estate lady, scouting out homes we could rent with an option to buy.

Renting with an option to buy was Dad's idea. For Dad, it wasn't so much an option to buy the house, but more an option to quit his job if things didn't work out.

We finally found and moved into an old, but newly painted, two-story farm house in acceptable condition. Behind the house were two long sheds that at one time housed egg-laying chickens. The house was a white, wood frame, square building with blue trim, set back from the main road. Upstairs were three bedrooms. That meant Harv and I each had our own room. I had a picture-postcard view. Mom pointed out that from my bedroom window I could see cornfields, apple orchards, woods, streams, a lake, and off in the distance a large billboard advertising our previous residence, the Hillside Motel.

I know I should have been pleased, but I was crabby. I missed my friends in Southfield.

Our first big family debate was about putting a mezuzah on the front door panel. Harv, Mom, and Dad insisted that we put one up. I was against it, arguing that a mezuzah was a sure giveaway. My friends would be curious about the unusual ornament and would badger me until I told, or they would ask their parents who would figure it out. In my mind, having a mezuzah by the door could even mean being dropped from basketball.

Basketball is my main sport. It's not just that I am tall for my age. I am good at it. As soon as Coach Stumpf saw me ball-handling in gym class, he approached me personally to ask if I would play for the team. The next day, I was at practice.

Before each practice and each game, Coach Stumpf had us kneel and say a short prayer, often starting the ritual with a defiant little pep talk: "There may be some godless intellectuals in Washington who deem our humble act of homage illegal, but I say to hell with the atheist lobby, the guys on my team pray before they play! Anybody object to that?" After Stumpf's speech, we spent about 10 seconds in silent prayer. I didn't like the idea. I had never had to pray prior to basketball practice before but, naturally, I kept my mouth shut. That was no problem. After all, it was a silent prayer.

When I told Harv about it, he wanted to know whether the atheist lobby was in the front or the back of the building. I had to explain to him that the atheist lobby wasn't a place, but a group of people trying to influence Congress. I pretended to be smart, but I had just learned that in Social Studies.

We settled the mezuzah question by painting it the same blue color as the door panel. It is hardly noticeable. Both my parents kiss it on the way in, just like they always have, but I never do. Harv kisses it, too. That should have clued me in right away that the kid would want a Bar Mitzvah.

The first time my new friend Bobby Olson came by, I was terrified that he'd notice the slanted stick on the door frame and ask embarrassing questions. Bobby lived in a rundown mobile home, in a shabby trailer court near the railroad tracks. Bobby never even looked up. But that didn't reassure me much. Every time someone came over, I had the same worry. So far, I've been lucky. Nobody's noticed our mezuzah.

The next big hurdle was getting through the holidays. At the time Dad got the job, the High Holidays were coming up, but we'd arranged to move in just after Yom Kippur, so that was taken care of. Fortunately, most Jewish holidays can be celebrated in the home. Every Friday evening, Mom continued to light candles and we shared Shabbat dinner together.

Behind our house is a small woods, very convenient for building a sukkah. We didn't dare. But I'm getting ahead of myself.

Dad was right about one thing. It wasn't easy switching from office supplies to farm equipment. For one thing, even if you have absolutely no concept of what you are doing, office supplies are rarely dangerous. The worst you can get is a paper cut. Not so with farm equipment. Farm equipment is extremely hazardous. The machines have moving parts that stick out all over the place: sliding beams, churning gears, and sharp blades that swing wildly about, every which way. There was so much to learn, and Dad was starting from Square One. He didn't know a disk harrow from a manure spreader. Every night, he took catalogues, with pictures of the mammoth, ridiculous-looking red and green contraptions, to bed with him, trying to memorize what each one was for and how it worked.

For the first few months, learning the equipment was so overwhelming, none of us took the Santa "clause" very seriously. That's what Dad called it, "the Santa clause." He said every contract had a hidden clause, his was the Santa clause.

Dad called himself the fat clown in the red suit,

41

or the Jolly Red Giant. We all regarded Santa as a comic, make-believe figure, with no particular religious meaning, until one cold Monday morning when our viewpoint abruptly changed.

It came as unhappy news that Uphill County was one of the most impoverished areas of the State. Kids from the poorer districts came to school in patched-up, too long or too short clothing. Although Southfield had a substantial "disadvantaged" Black population, personally I never knew any kids as poor as those around here.

For the first few weeks, everyone in the family was amazed at the poverty around us. Carlos who came to school with mismatched socks; the lady in the torn blue sweater who picked through the discarded fruit behind the market; the long lines outside the Unemployment Office; the vagrants who accosted you on the street for handouts; the tumbledown, shack-houses in the poor section they called Shantytown; the dingy trailer park where the Olson's lived.

The condition of our neighbors was brought literally to our doorstep one cold Monday morning about three weeks after we moved in.

A middle-aged woman in a tattered gray coat rapped at our back door. The woman told Mom that she used to feed the chickens and gather eggs for the people who lived here before us. Mom explained that we didn't have any chickens. The woman pleaded that she had three young children to care for. She offered to do anything: laundry, scrub floors, cook, iron, general cleaning, even paint walls. She was desperate. Mom couldn't hire her, but fished $10 from her purse to give the woman. The woman said that she had walked three miles and had no way of getting to a store. She asked if Mom could spare any food. Mom gave the woman a few potatoes, some groceries, plus the $10. The woman left, but Mom couldn't stop thinking about her.

That evening, at dinner, Mom told us what happened. "I've been thinking," she said. "Why not take Dad's Santa Claus role seriously?"

Mom had a proposal. Instead of merely giving the poor children a smile and candy during Christmas, Santa could distribute coupons that could be exchanged for nice gifts. She had it all figured out. We would collect old toys, clothes, etc. At Christmas time, we would distribute them as gifts in exchange for the coupons.

It happened that we were invited to visit the Olafsen's the following Sunday. Mom used the occasion to present her idea. Mrs. Beatrice Olafsen took to it at once, and expanded upon the coupon scheme.

Between Mom, Mrs. Olafsen and her friends, a committee was formed. Mom was appointed the chairwoman.

Harv and I were drafted into this new Brigade. This time, Mom was the General. Beatrice Vander Olafsen persuaded her husband to allot one of the FarMich equipment garages as a storehouse. The Coupon Exchange project was soon underway.

Mom made the rounds to the Salvation Army, the St. Vincent De Paul Society, and the Purple Heart, and persuaded each of them to cooperate. Beatrice Olafsen enlisted the participation of the PTA, the Welfare Office, and the Unemployment Office. Each agreed to supply lists of their neediest clients. It was Harvey's and my task to enter names into the computer. Most of the agency lists were provided on floppy disks, which made collecting the information easier.

Donations started as a trickle, but as word of our campaign spread, the flow increased to a steady stream. Families donated old toys, used clothing, and household goods. Stores donated food. The laundry, cleaners, and shoe repair shops donated unclaimed items. We received gifts of used appliances and computers. I donated my Legos. Harv donated my never-worn red swimming trunks.

Volunteers poured in to help and they were all kept busy. People were needed to man the phones, collect donations, and pass out flyers. Contributed items had to be inspected, sorted, cleaned, and repaired before they were displayed. The storehouse

had to be cleaned, outfitted with tables, and decorated. Hay bales were covered with long stretches
of brown paper and converted to counter tops. Volunteers became known as Santa's Helpers.

Harv acquired a fan. She must have thought he
was cute. Her name was Tammi Carmichael. She
volunteered to be one of Santa's Helpers. She was
in Harv's class. Tammi pretended to visit our house
so Harv could help her with her homework, but she
always brought along a pile of CDs that they ended
up listening to. Mom disapproved of Tammi because
while she was only eleven years old, she wore bright
red lipstick and nail polish. Harv persuaded Tammi
to give many of her CDs to the Exchange.

I hadn't made many friends, so far. Occasion-
ally, Bobby and I got together. Usually, I hung out
with my basketball teammates, but I would hardly
call them my friends. We had practically nothing in
common. The guys on the basketball team were
mainly farm boys whose idea of fun was making
animal noises behind the teacher's back.

One time, Mr. Swensen was putting an algebra
problem on the board, and Luke LaPorte in the back
of the room let out a long "mooo." Some kids in the
class snickered. Mr. Swensen turned around and
glared at the class. He must have caught a smirk on
Luke's face, or knew he'd be the likely culprit, because he kicked him out of class. Swensen must

have called Luke's parents, because for the following week Luke was too sore to sit on the bench; forget about going to practice.

With the backing of the PTA, Hilltop High sponsored a Coupon Campaign Poster Contest. Every poster entered was posted somewhere around town. Gift Coupons were designed in the high school graphics lab and printed in the high school print shop.

I put up a Coupon Exchange poster in the locker room, but none of my basketball buddies wanted anything to do with Santa's Helpers. The in-crowd clique at Hilltop High, which included all the popular kids and almost everyone in varsity athletics, shunned the poorer kids like Bobby Olson whom they called "scummies."

Coupon Exchange Day was set for the day after Christmas, called Boxing Day, which according to British tradition is celebrated by passing out gift boxes to the lower classes. By Halloween, almost everyone had heard of the Campaign. Posters adorned every storefront window and in every part of town you could see the orange flyers blowing about in the wind littering the streets. Volunteers worked in shifts. Piles of gifts began to accumulate in Olafsen's equipment barn.

With PTA support, kids were encouraged to contribute some of their Halloween loot to the campaign. I was way too old to go trick-or-treating, but Harv dressed up as Robin Hood, and adopted the traits of his make-believe character by giving away all his candy to the Gift Exchange.

The first week in November, six inches of snow fell. All ugliness disappeared. Even the scruffiest, dingiest landmarks were covered beneath a clean, soft, white blanket of snow.

From my window, I watched as white snowy mists blew across the fields. Snowdrift mounds piled up against hedges and fences. Traffic on the main road slowed to a stop, and school was suspended.

Harv helped me shovel the walk, the wind stinging our faces. When we went back in, our house felt warm and cozy, but I couldn't help but wonder about Bobby Olson's family in their drafty trailer or the poor families in Shantytown.

For me, the freezing weather had its compensations. I went sledding, ice skating, and skiing. My friends invited me to go tobogganing and ice fishing, which I had never done before. But as much as I enjoyed the ice and snow, I was glad that I had a nice warm house to return to at night.

In his Santa costume, Dad made a splendid Jolly Red Giant. You could easily spot him a mile away stomping along in his bright red suit, his tall black boots looking like exclamation marks in the snow.

At the Community Hall, kids lined up to have their picture taken with Dad, and you could see they got a big kick out of sitting on Santa's lap. And Dad got his share of kicks, too, as the kids climbed their way up and down.

Little Luanne Mauler tugged at Santa's fluffy white beard, which was fake, but her brother George punched Santa's big round tummy, which was not. Dad let out a howl that bounced George right off his lap, and onto the floor.

George jumped up and yelled, "Hey, cool! You're a real Santa, aren't ya?"

Despite a few kicks and punches, Dad liked being Jolly St. Nick, proving again and again that he could bellow his "ho-ho-ho" as heartily as any Santa anywhere.

Between Thanksgiving and Christmas, Dad made dozens of appearances as Santa. Dad made sure that all the poorer kids got Gift Coupons.

Dad wasn't alone. Mom and her work teams distributed coupons to the Unemployment Office, the Welfare Office, and the public schools. These agencies redistributed the coupons, in turn, to their needy clientele.

Throughout the season, the Coupon Campaign gathered momentum. The storehouse, humming with volunteers, more and more resembled a factory. Because of Santa's Helpers, Mom and Dad became minor celebrities, and attended several holiday parties that served as benefits for the Exchange. Our parents, being non-drinkers, were appalled and disgusted by the conduct of some of the other guests who deliberately set out to become highly intoxicated and sometimes became physically sick.

About two weeks before Christmas, Tammi Carmichael asked Harv if she could see our tree. Harv was a little shocked. But, true to form, he answered honestly, saying, "We don't have one."

Tammi was disappointed because she had decorated some CD disks with paint and glitter to hang on our tree. Harvey told her that he would hang them on the Coupon Exchange tree, but Tammi was still disappointed. We weren't unique in not having a tree. Several kids in our school were Jehovah's Witnesses or other denominations that don't celebrate Christmas. Even so, the incident made me nervous.

Harvey was in for a real shock when he attended Tammi's holiday party. I guess he expected to play Pin the Tail on the Donkey, like we usually did at children's parties, but Mrs. Carmichael had other plans. She thought the children were old enough to play a game called Spin the Bottle. After she explained the game, eleven-year-old Harv told Mrs. Carmichael that he had to go home.

Harvey claimed he was feeling too sick to play and that the doctor had warned him that he was highly contagious. Mrs. Carmichael must have believed him, because she got very flustered and agreed he should go home. Tammi cried as Harv zippered up his coat, and made for the door. As soon as he was away from their house, Harv pretended to spit three times into the snow . Harvey did that sometimes as a display of disgust.

On Boxing Day, Mom and her Helpers opened the Exchange. To minimize crowding, patrons were admitted in groups. All day long, convoys of yellow school buses spewing white vapor from their tailpipes could be seen shuttling indigent families to and from the FarmMich Storage garage. Hundreds of visitors took advantage of the Exchange. Each coupon could be exchanged for one gift. Streams of smiling men, women and children emerged from the mammoth building carrying TVs, VCRs, microwaves, computers, toasters, jackets, shoes, toys, CDs, books, games, bicycles, and kitchenware.

Because some poor families lived off the school bus routes, Dad drove a large white truck, with a big picture of Sir Claus and his reindeer painted on the side, to service those unable to travel. Harv and I went with him. Our first stop was the trailer park, where the Olsons lived.

To spare him embarrassment, we took Bobby Olson along with us in the truck. Dad drove in his Santa suit, the radio blaring Jingle Bells. Soon after we entered the gate, the truck was surrounded by cheering children waving coupons. Bobby, Harvey, and I organized the throng of coupon holders into a mannerly line.

On the way home, Dad asked Harvey and me what we did this day.

"We delivered presents to the poor." I said.

"That's not all," said Dad. "We performed a mitzvah." The word "mitzvah" got Harv going.

"Dad, I want a Bar Mitzvah," he wailed. "Jeff had a Bar Mitzvah."

"Harvey, you can't have a Bar Mitzvah, and you know why, so quit whining," I said.

Harvey began to sulk, but he shut up.

The Coupon Exchange was a huge success. At the end of the day, virtually nothing was left. Even some of the hay bales had been carted off.

That evening, Mr. Olafsen drove us back to his house for a big celebration. He was all praise and compliments, saying that he knew Mr. Kinder was the real McCoy the moment he laid eyes on him. He thanked us over and over again, saying how proud he was of us all. I had to explain to Harv what "the real McCoy" meant.

At one point, Mr. O. asked my brother Harvey, "What was the hardest part of being Santa's Helper?"

"Getting Santa's big, black boots on and off!" Harv blurted out. Everybody laughed.

Mr. O. wanted to know, "And how did you accomplish that?"

Harvey described it exactly the way we did it. "Dad lay stretched out on the bed," he said, "and both Jeff and I had to push and pull with all our might to get those boots on and off." Again everyone laughed and clapped their hands.

Hanukkah was late that year. It started the day before Christmas. During Hanukkah, we avoided inviting kids over because of the menorah. The menorah was placed in an obscure corner of the kitchen counter on a sheet of aluminum foil. On each of the eight nights of Hanukkah, when Dad came home from work, we said the blessings and lit one additional candle. The menorah was always shielded from the window. Harv suggested we put a wreath on the door to further avoid suspicion, but the rest of us agreed that would be going overboard. Personally, I think Harv was being sarcastic.

The one thing I do miss in Hillside are Jewish girls. The only appealing girl in the entire high school is Corrine McQuid. In fact, Corrine is undeniably the prettiest girl in the school. She is blond, she has blue eyes, and she is a cheerleader. Luke LaPorte told everybody that Corrine is his personal property and warned all the guys to stay away. I caught her smiling at me a few times, but I was way too shy to talk to her. Anyway, Corrine is always surrounded by Luke and his basketball pals. Under Luke's orders, they cordon her off and guard her as they do our basket on the playing court.

Corrine may be attractive on the outside, but she is definitely not my type. She smokes, she drinks, and she persuades Luke to shoplift cosmetics for her from the drug store where he works after school. Another thing that bugs me is her speech. Her language is terrible. She is very crude and vulgar. Her English is worse than the migrant workers, and they're Mexican. But I do have to admit, she's very pretty.

To everyone's relief, Dad is doing exceptionally well. His sales figures are good. He made four major sales of expensive equipment to new customers, which really pleased Mr. O.

Dad is a member of the Optimists Club, the Chamber of Commerce, the Rotary, and a half-dozen other civic organizations. At these meetings he often hears anti-Jewish jokes and other remarks that he repeats for us. It makes us all very uncomfortable to hear Dad's anti-Semitic stories. Thank goodness, no one has directly asked us about our religion.

That's probably because the one religion everyone in Hillside practices is Politeness. It's a good thing that in Hillside, it just isn't polite to ask people about their money or their religious beliefs. Living here, I feel like the Marranos of Spain during the Middle Ages. I may not be dodging the Inquisition, but I am still a secret Jew. Pretending to be something that I am not is rotten. It's miserable to fear being found out, or worry that my reactions will give me away.

Harv has been squawking again about having a Bar Mitzvah. If Harvey has a public Bar Mitzvah, then the jig is up. Everybody will know we're Jewish, and that we've been lying to them all along. I told Harv that if he wants a Bar Mitzvah, he should have it in Southfield where we used to live. But no, he says he's tired of living a lie, and, besides, all his friends are here. He says he's coming out of hiding.

I told Harv that I am just as sick of being under-cover as he is, but we've both heard Dad's anti-Jewish stories. I also know what my friends think about Jews. Hillside doesn't have any Jews, I tell him, but it's obvious they have a bad opinion of us. Anyway, I ask him how he reacts when someone says, "I jewed her out of $5," or, "He's being a real Jew about it!"

Harv has no answer, but of this he is sure: he is coming out of hiding, he is going to have a Bar Mitzvah, and it is going to be in Hillside. Talk like that is dangerous.

As adamant as he is to have his Bar Mitzvah, I am just as determined to talk him out of it. I challenge him, "Who's gonna teach you? You don't have the slightest idea how much there is to learn. There's no way you'll learn the blessings, the *Maftir,* and the Haftorah.

"The closest Rabbi lives in an igloo 200 miles away." Of course that's not true, but I am out to discourage him as much as possible.

"I've got two whole years before my birthday. I'll learn it!" he cries.

Now I really let him have it. "So, you want Dad to lose his job, you want me to be kicked off varsity basketball, just so you can have your stupid, selfish Bar Mitzvah?"

He begins to cry. I feel bad. I don't mean to make him cry but, at the same time I don't want him to blow our cover.

Harvey goes to our parents, as I knew he would, and they talk him out of it, as I knew they would. Once you begin living a lie, it just ain't that easy to come clean.

As I said before, my life mainly centered around basketball. Basketball was big at Hilltop High and I got to play in the Homecoming Game. That was a great game. We played against Hayfield, our traditional rivals. It was a very close game. In the last five seconds of the game, I scored a 3-pointer. My parents and Harv were in the stands. Everybody was cheering their heads off when I scored the winning basket. The Hilltop kids rushed the court, and hoisted me on their shoulders. I'll never forget it. I was the town hero. Everybody loved me.

In the locker room afterwards, I remember wondering, "What would all these people think if they knew I was Jewish and had been just pretending to be one of them all this time?" Harv's Bar Mitzvah idea could ruin everything.

Harvey, though, had no such worries. Of all my fans, he was the proudest. He enjoyed telling everyone, "Jeff's my brother, you know." He was continuously asking his friends, "Did you see that shot when my brother Jeff sank the 3-pointer?" Or, he might point me out in the mall, "See that guy over there? He's my brother, Jeff, the one who won the game against Hayfield."

Frankly, I found his bragging embarrassing. But no matter how often I told Harv to cut it out, he kept it up.

Many team members didn't like my being friends with Bobby Olson, or the fact that I promoted the Coupon Exchange. They accused me of being on the side of the scummies. I wasn't even aware there were sides.

The Hayfield game was probably the only reason why Luke invited me to his private New Year's Eve bash. Luke's parents were away for the weekend, and he threw a huge party. The party was supposed to be held in his basement, but it spilled over into the entire house, and into the barn. The next morning they even found beer cans in the silo. Getting drunk on beer seemed to be everyone's idea of a good time. The only reason I stayed was to be one of the guys. Luke and most of his pals, including Corrine McQuid, were already drunk. I don't like beer, but I pretended to sip from my can. I resented my reputation as a "goody two-shoes."

Around midnight, Luke fell asleep on the floor with his arm around a basketball. To my surprise, Corrine came over and sat by me on the sofa. I felt myself getting very nervous and flustered by her closeness. She smelled like perfumed beer, which made me slightly nauseous. She leaned over, and said in a kind of thick whisper, "Jeffrey, honey, I know where the LaPorte's hide their liquor. You c'mon and help me jimmy the liquor cab'net open, then me n' you can really get high."

"No way!" I tell her. I was thinking that this girl is crazy. How does she even have the nerve to ask me something like that? Then she comes up with an even crazier idea.

"Hey Jeffrey, let's you 'n me check out the bedroom drawers for jewelry, money, and stuff. Nobody'll know it was us that made off with it."

Again, I refused. I could see that Corrine was getting irritated with me.

"Do you want to go outside for a walk?" I asked, hoping the cold air might sober her up.

"Nah," she said, "You don't have no weed on ya, do ya, Jeff?"

When I said "no" to that, too, she said, "Damn you, Jeff, you ain't no fun at all!" and got up and walked away. Drunk or not, that conversation cured me of the last little bit of interest I had in Corrine McQuid.

Of all the changes that I went through at Hillside, the weirdest was my school grades. School suddenly became much easier for me. I am no great student, but Hilltop High was a snap compared to Southfield.

I wasn't the smartest kid in my class, but for the first time in my life I was in the top ten percent. It's amazing what a big difference something small like reading the chapter or doing your homework can make in your grade point average. For the first time in my life, kids were asking me for help with their homework. Luke's mother even offered to pay me to tutor her son in algebra. I told her I couldn't accept tutoring money. The truth was, I was having too much trouble with algebra myself to tutor Luke. It's funny though, how just being asked can build your confidence. It actually made me proud of getting better grades.

Another thing. Getting better marks made me view college differently. In our family, it was presumed that Harv and I would go to college. In my mind, however, the word college was always followed by the word basketball. I literally dreamed of playing college basketball. Taking classes in college hadn't entered my mind. For the first time, I began to wonder what subjects I might take in college.

Dad sent off e-mails practically every night telling Uncle Yoav about his new job, about his adventures playing Santa, and about the success of the Coupon Exchange. Aunt Tzippi translated at the other end.

Then came the bombshell.

Without warning, Uncle Yoav announced that in May, he would be touring the United States, and he would be making a special trip up to Hillside to visit our family.

Of course, Dad hadn't told Uncle Yoav anything about the fact that we were hiding our religion. How could he? More than anyone, Uncle Yoav was extremely proud of being Jewish. He would never understand.

I panicked. I was convinced that when Uncle Yoav arrived everything would fall apart. Everybody knows that the worst thing in the world is a liar. On TV, if the great detective or a brilliant attorney can show that the suspect has lied about the smallest detail, that's proof positive that he committed the horrible murder.

Mentally, I began to prepare myself for disaster. Everybody hates a liar. I've heard it all my life: "The one thing I can't stand is a liar," or, "I would have forgiven him if he hadn't lied about it." Hillside is a very small town. As soon as Uncle Yoav shows up, everyone will know that our whole family is nothing but a bunch of liars.

I began having bad dreams about it. In one dream, I am alone on the basketball court. Everybody I ever knew is in the stands, and they are all chanting, "Liar! Liar! Liar! Liar!" I try to escape, but the crowd surrounds me, and blocks the exits. Then the floor turns into a Velcro carpet and the bottoms of my shoes become Velcro hooks. I struggle, but I can't lift a foot. The more I pull, the more tightly I am locked in place, until I can't move at all. At that point, Coach Stumpf appears and gives his brief pre-game speech. Everyone kneels down around me. But this time, instead of praying silently, everyone has to pray out loud to their God.

In another dream, I am sitting in Mr. Swensen's class wearing only my red swimming trunks. Everyone else is bundled up in their winter clothes. The room is bitter cold. I am shivering and freezing to death, but no one cares. In fact, they're all laughing at me. The funny thing is that when I woke up from that dream, I actually was cold. I had the chills.

Mom and Harv don't seem very concerned about Uncle Yoav's visit. They even seem to be looking forward to it. I try to explain my fears to them, but they refuse to understand. They think it's about admitting that we are Jewish. I keep telling them that it's all about being a liar. Dad, on the other hand, seems as worried as I am.

We have a major family discussion about my concerns. Mom asks if any of us have actually denied that we are Jewish. No. None of us have. So, we haven't really lied, she points out, we just never told anyone what our faith is. That stops me cold. She's right. Dad played Santa, but that wasn't denying his Judaism.

Dad and I are relieved. In the end we agree that it would be better if we ourselves announce who we are before Uncle Yoav shows up. And the sooner, the better. I tell myself I'll tell the guys tomorrow.

",This is great!" shouts Harv. "Now, I can have a Bar Mitzvah!" And he starts in again singing Hava Nagillah.

"No, you can't," I say. "Who will teach you your Torah portion, and where can you hold the service? There are no synagogues in Hillside, or did you forget? Of course," I remind him, "you can always have your Bar Mitzvah in Southfield." This makes Harv cry again. He runs to his room. Mom gets angry with me, but all I did was just tell the truth.

"Why do you have to upset him?" she scolds. Then she follows Harv into his room.

The next day, before basketball practice, I announce, "Hey, guys, my Uncle Yoav from Israel will be visiting me next month."

"That's cool."

That was it.

Doug Feena said, "That's cool." And then he and the other guys go right back to talking about the usual stuff: sports, cars, teachers, girls, and the particular reasons each of them is being grounded this week.

Harv decided to make his announcement during Show and Tell in his homeroom class. That evening he described how he stood up and said, "Next month, my Uncle Yoav is coming to visit. He lives on a kibbutz in Israel.

"My teacher, Mrs. Agula, asked the class, 'Who knows where Israel is?' One hand flies up. It's Joel Johanssen. Joel will guess at any question whether he knows the answer or not. 'Yes, Joel?'

'It's in Arizona.'

'No, Joel,' she corrected him, 'Israel is a country in the Middle East.

'Harvey, can you tell the class what a kibbutz is?'

'It's a big farm that's run like a summer camp,' I told her.

'Yes, Harvey, I suppose it is, for the children. But here, we call it a collective farm, because the people who live on the kibbutz share the equipment and share all the work.'

"I thought for sure she'd ask me if I was Jewish," Harv said, "but she just smiled and told me to sit down."

The big surprise came when Dad told Mr. Olafsen. Dad was very nervous. He saw Vander O. in the machine shop, and tried to appear casual as he approached his boss.

"My brother-in-law will be visiting from Israel next month," Dad said real nonchalantly.

"Yes, I know," Mr. O. said, just as nonchalantly.

"You know?!" Dad said, amazed.

"Sure, Yoav and I have been in touch for more than a year discussing major purchases of farm equipment, not only for Yoav's kibbutz, but for his entire kibbutz federation."

"I had no idea!" Dad said, now really dazed.

"I know that, too. My problem was that I didn't speak Hebrew and Yoav didn't know English. That's where you came in."

"But you never asked if I spoke Hebrew."

"First of all, it's against the law for me to ask those kinds of questions. But I already knew that you did."

"How did you know?"

"Yoav told me. He told me you needed a job. I told him I'd give you an interview."

"You hired me because I spoke Hebrew?"

"That wasn't the only reason. You made a good

impression. I liked your style. I decided to take a chance on you. I felt you could do the job, and I was right."

"What about needing a Santa Claus?"

"That was just a cover story."

"Why did you need a cover story?"

"Because your wife warned me that if you knew that Yoav had set this up, you never would have accepted my offer. So, I invented that story about needing a Santa. Pretty creative, huh?"

"So, you didn't really dread being the official town Santa?"

"Heck, I loved being Santa. I was jealous every minute that you were in that red suit."

"So, my Santa days are over?"

"Sorry, Mr. Kinder, but Old St. Nick is taking his sleigh back." Dad walked away like he was in a trance.

We had intended to go to Bubbie's house for our annual *seders*, but Bubbie and Zaydie came up to Hillside instead. That was Mr. Olafsen's idea. He had always wanted to attend a real Jewish seder.

Mr. Olafsen brought his wife Beatrice and his four children. Harvey said the Four Questions, and Honey Olafsen, Vander's six-year-old daughter, found the *afikomen*, which she traded for a Made-in-Israel dreidle.

For those eight days, I had to bring enough matzoh to school for the whole team.

The Hillside elementary school is usually locked tight on weekends, but this Saturday morning the school auditorium was packed. It was Harvey's big day. All of Harvey's friends, including Tammi Carmichael, armed with candy, were stationed in the front row within throwing distance of their target. Also in the front row, but off to one side, sat most of our family, including Uncle Bernie, who usually winters in Florida, in jail. Uncle Yoav, Aunt Tzippi, and my two cousins were seated right behind him. Many friends from Southfield came, too. Also in attendance were Mr. Olafsen and Dad's co-workers, Harv's teachers and most of the town's population.

Few people wanted to miss it. Hillside had never had a Bar Mitzvah before.

The town had made a special effort to change the Hillside Elementary School auditorium into a synagogue. Religious items, including a real Sefer Torah, were brought in for the occasion. Local carpenters built a *bima*, a raised platform, and an ark to hold the Torah. The town did a fine job decorating. White fabric embroidered with Jewish symbols covered the bima, and a beautiful blue velvet drape wrapped the ark.

Harvey looked so grown-up, up there on the bima, standing next to Rabbi Mintz and Dad's old pals. It made me realize how much can change in two years.

I graduated Hilltop High. Now I'm playing basketball for Michigan State. Diets must work because Harvey and Dad both look much thinner. Harvey must have grown more than a foot. Almost overnight, he became a tough opponent when we play one-on-one basketball in the driveway.

Oh, in case you're wondering how Harvey mastered the blessings, the Maftir, and his Haftorah: he learned most of it from a computer program on a CD-ROM that Uncle Yoav sent him from Israel. Plus just a little coaching from the Hillside town Santa.

You should have been there when Harvey, wearing his tallit and white kippah, completed his Haftorah, and stepped off the bima.

The crowd went wild!

The
Three Wishes
of
Nathan the Wise

Rabbi Michael Datz *was born in Houston, Texas in 1956. He grew up on a steady diet of television sitcoms.*

After obtaining his law degree from the University of Houston, Rabbi Datz attended Hebrew Union College–Jewish Institute of Religion in Jerusalem and Cincinnati. Ordained as a reform Rabbi in 1987, he has served congregations in Johannesburg, South Africa and Curacao, Netherlands Antilles. He is currently the spiritual leader of Temple B'rith Sholom in Springfield, Illinois.

Rabbi Datz writes a regular column for the local newspaper, as well as annual Hanukkah plays for children.

In this, his first published short story, Rabbi Datz brings a Jewish twist to the age-old adage — Be careful what you ask for, you just may get it.

Rabbi Datz and his wife, Josephine, have two children.

It was already nearly noon, the first day after the start of the schools' Winter Holidays. At least that's what they called it at the synagogue: "The Winter Holidays." But, as far as Nathan could tell, it just looked like the plain ol' Christmas holidays. The advertisements in the newspaper never said, "Just fifteen more shopping days 'til the Winter Holidays." The department store Santa NEVER asked, "And what would *you* like for the Winter Holidays?" And, at public school, the choir NEVER sang "Winter Holiday Carols."

Once, when he asked his Hebrew teacher, Mrs. Lipsky, about it, she just smiled, and said, "Well, now, Nathan, how would that sound if we said that Hebrew School was letting out for Christmas vacation?" Then she winked at him.

He wasn't completely sure what it meant when Mrs. Lipsky winked at him. Did it mean that she understood how he felt about Christmas? Or maybe even that she felt the same way?

When he was little, Nathan always wished his family could have Christmas like so many of his friends. All the lights and decorations looked so beautiful. His own family only celebrated Hanukkah. He liked it and all — each member of the family had their own *Hanukkiah* which they lit for eight nights — but, even with *latkes* and playing *dreidle*, it just didn't seem quite as good as Christmas.

Today, his soccer coach asked him to explain about Hanukkah to his buddies on the team. Since his Social Studies teacher at school had asked him a week earlier to make a presentation about Hanukkah to his class, he was already prepared with an answer:

"Well, like a long time ago there were these Jewish guys called the Macabees. And they had a war against the Greeks...."

"The *geeks*?" one of his teammates asked.

"Not the geeks, you geek. The *Greeks,*" Nathan corrected him. "Anyway, the Greeks wouldn't let the Jews practice their religion, and they wanted us to play sports without clothes on, like they did...."

"You mean these Greeks played sports without their clothes on — like NAKED? Cool." Another teammate interrupted, "If we could play soccer that way, I bet a lot more girls would come watch us play."

"Yeah, but who's gonna sponsor the team if we're not wearing T-shirts with some company's name on them?" a third teammate asked.

"Hey, c'mon, guys. This is a serious story I'm tryin' to tell you," Nathan protested. "Okay, so the Jews had a war against the Greeks, and this fellow, Judah Macabee, led them into battle. And the Jews won, even though they were way outnumbered. So now we celebrate Hanukkah, and we remember about religious freedom and all that good stuff," Nathan finished his speech.

"So what's all that got to do with Christmas?" one of his buddies asked.

"Exactly nothing," Nathan answered quickly. "The two holidays just come at the same time. Only we light candles, and play games, and eat potato pancakes. Here, I'll show you."

Nathan's mother had made potato latkes for his class at school. Since there was a little kitchen at the clubhouse, Nathan had thought he would save some of the batter and fry it for his soccer team. He took out the bowl of batter which his mother had left for him, but — yech! — it had all turned into brown and green mush.

"We're gonna eat that stuff?" his buddies all shouted in unison.

"Well, I thought so." Nathan scooped a handful of the batter. "But maybe not." Nathan smiled, and then slung a glob of the pancake mix at a friend who was standing next to him. Splat! It landed on his face, and dribbled down his cheeks. Everybody laughed, especially when his friend took a handful of the gook and slung it back at Nathan. Soon everybody was having a potato batter fight. Spew! Splat! Splush!

When he arrived home that evening, his sister was the first to greet him.

"What happened?!"

"Food fight at soccer practice. We called it Laser Latkes."

"Charming. Mom's gonna be mad. The only present you're gonna get for Hanukkah is a hot shower and a bar of soap. Too bad I'm using the bathroom right now. And I'll probably be in there for another hour, at least," she smiled.

As Nathan looked at himself in the mirror — what a mess he was — he thought that that was another thing about Christmas. His friends got so many presents; all spread out under a Christmas tree. For several years, he had begged his parents for a tree, but all they would say was, "Absolutely not." His father would add, "Son, you can't have everything." His mother would then give him a hug, and gently remind him, "Honey, it's not our holiday. We're Jewish and sometimes that means being different. If we did Christmas, it would be like telling a lie. Someday, when you're older, I hope you'll understand."

"When I'm older, I'll probably be handing that same line to my son," is what Nathan wanted to say. "And I still won't understand why!" Of course, he didn't dare say that.

The truth was, as he grew older, he did understand a little better, even if it wasn't always so easy to explain it to his teammates and classmates. Hanukkah, he had decided, was beautiful, in its own quiet way. But, deep down, he still kinda wished he could have Christmas, too. Despite what his father said, he would have *liked* to have everything. He bet Mrs. Lipsky would have understood.

Mrs. Lipsky was his favorite teacher at the synagogue. She always seemed completely honest. She was sorta short, and sorta round. Her hair was sorta red, and sorta fluffy. She always looked warm and cozy. She laughed a great deal, and her eyes danced in a strange kind of way. He imagined that she would make a great department store Santa, although he wasn't sure if Jews could do that kind of thing, or if Mrs. Lipsky could even get down a chimney. But if she ever got stuck, he figured she would probably be pretty jolly about the situation. She'd probably just pull out her cellular phone and call the fire department for help. They'd get a giant plunger and pop ol' Mrs. Lipsky out of the chimney. Pow! She'd go soaring, yelling, "Ho! Ho! Ho!" and probably order a pizza on her cell phone as she prepared to land. That's the kind of neat lady Mrs. Lipsky was.

Nathan suddenly snapped back to reality. He better get cleaned up fast, before his mother saw him.

It was nearly noon when he awoke the next morning. That's because Nathan had slept late. And that was because Nathan had stayed up very late the night before, watching old television shows. After all, it was the first day of the Winter Holidays.

The house was very quiet. Nathan suddenly remembered that his mother had taken his brother and sister to do a few errands, and then to see a movie. It was only a few more nights until Hanukkah, so maybe Mom was going to shop for presents. It was also a Friday morning. That would mean a stop to buy flowers, and another stop at the bakery for *challahs* for Shabbat dinner that evening.

He did some quick arithmetic in his head. "Wow!" Nathan figured he had at least another two or three hours to be **HOME ALONE!** What a luxury.

His father would not be around, reminding him to study his Torah reading for his Bar Mitzvah lesson with the Rabbi. He knew he probably *should* listen more to the Bar Mitzvah tape. But it was usually just too tempting to put a different cassette — music he really liked — into the Walk Man.

His mother would not be around, telling him to read a book instead of watching so much television. If only someone would invent a remote control to turn the pages of the book. Better yet, invent something that would read his books for him. It was just so much more fun to channel surf on the TV.

Besides, he was only allowed to watch TV six days a week. Most of his friends — even his Jewish friends — watched every day of the week. But his parents had recently decided that there would be no TV on Shabbat. Not playing soccer on Friday nights was hard enough. But no television either!? His mother said they should rather spend the time talking to each other, instead. Now *that* was a good reason to read a book! The thought of talking to his sister all night....

At his parents' suggestion, he did try talking to his sister — once. Just once. The conversation went something like:

"Hey...."

"Hey...."

"What's goin' on?"

"Nothing."

"Oh. OK. Uh...your hair looks good."

"You never compliment me on my hair. What do you want? I hope you're not thinking I'm going to help you with your homework," his sister said, angrily.

"No way. Why would I ask for help from a veggie-brain like you? It's just that Mom and Dad said we should talk to each other more," he explained.

"Uh huh. That sounds like a good idea." Then the phone rang. "It's for me!" she yelled. "I'll get it." His sister ran upstairs, and disappeared into her room. And that was the end of that. Nathan figured he probably wouldn't see her again for about six months.

He suddenly remembered once more that it was Winter Break and he was **HOME ALONE!** It was *so* great. His older sister would not be around to hog the bathroom when he really needed it. Needed it *bad.* Needed it *now.* All she ever did was stand in front of the mirror to put on makeup. What a pain!

And his younger brother would not be around to make a pest of himself. He was almost as big a pain as his sister. Yeah, he was a cute little kid; but he always wanted to crawl on Nathan's lap while Nathan was fooling around on the computer. And then he would start banging on the keyboard, just when Nathan was about to beat Mad Dog McRee.

It was bad enough, of course, when his little brother messed up one of Nathan's computer games. But that wasn't even the worst of it. Recently, he had completely wiped out one of Nathan's homework assignments. And not just any old assignment. It was for Miss Henderson's class.

Miss Henderson was his least favorite teacher. She was the opposite of Mrs. Lipsky. Where Mrs. Lipsky was round, Miss Henderson was thin as a Barbie doll. Where Mrs. Lipsky's eyes twinkled, Miss Henderson's flashed. Where Mrs. Lipsky loved to laugh, Miss Henderson loved to grimace. Mrs. Lipsky was also about twenty years older than Miss Henderson, but they both had the same colored auburn hair.

Miss Henderson always sat on a stool, with one leg crossed over the other. The one leg would swing back and forth, and she would dangle her high-heeled shoe from her toes. She also had a habit of running her hand through her hair, and giving it a little toss. Nathan was convinced that she would one day toss either her shoe or her hair right off — maybe even both at the same time — and they would land on Buster Carson, the biggest baby in the class. He imagined her sitting on her stool with one shoe on, looking just as bald as a department store dummy in a display window. Meanwhile, Buster would be crying, wondering why it was raining hair and shoes on him.

Miss Henderson taught History and Social Studies. It was in her class that Nathan had first explained about Hanukkah, and it was for her class that his mother had made latkes. Of course, being so skinny (in the school cafeteria she never ate anything but salads), Miss Henderson would only nibble a bit of latke. If she found out how much oil — good old high cholesterol oil — his mother fried the latkes in, she would probably have shriveled up and died.

Well, the day after his brother wiped out his homework on the computer, Nathan tried to explain the situation to Miss Henderson. Unfortunately, she was a no-nonsense kind of teacher and wasn't buying any of it.

"Young man," she began. "It's time you started taking responsibility for your assignments. I believe you're quite a soccer player, right? Suppose you played soccer with the same casual attitude as you approach your schoolwork. You'd still be sitting on the sidelines. You need to apply yourself more seriously to your Social Studies. I expect that assignment to be completed, and on my desk, the first day we come back from the Winter vacation."

Nathan had already heard Miss Henderson give variations of this same speech to several other classmates. About halfway through, his attention began to wander.

He imagined Miss Henderson sitting in a restaurant, one leg crossed over the other, her shoe dangling from her toes. He walked up to her and introduced himself. "Hi, I'm Nathan, and I'll be your waiter tonight. Are you familiar with our salad bar?"

Suddenly he noticed that Miss Henderson had a head of lettuce instead of red hair. Nathan pretended he was pouring salad dressing over her head.

"Would you like some croutons?"

"Why, yes, thank you."

"And some freshly ground pepper?"

"That would also be nice."

Nathan took out a pair of salad servers and began to toss Miss Henderson's hair. Her legs abruptly turned into long, thin franks and her shoe turned into a dachshund's face and began barking.

"Weiner Schnitzel?" he asked Miss Salad Henderson.

Nathan drifted back to reality once more. Wow!

Another two or three hours *HOME ALONE*! Nathan weighed his options....

His mother wanted him to read more because she herself loved to read so much. She always had a stack of four or five books by her bed. Hmmm! He could take out the book markers and move them around....

Or, he could put his Bar Mitzvah tape cassette into his father's car stereo and then turn it up to the highest volume....

Or, he could put glue into his sister's mascara bottle. Maybe it would make her eyelashes stick to her eyelids.... Better still, he could use the mascara to paint mustaches and black teeth on all those rock-star posters covering the walls of her bedroom.

Or, he could — no, he better leave his brother alone. He was just a little kid, after all, and he really didn't mean any harm.

Besides, his parents had a major rule that there was to be no fighting on Friday afternoons before Shabbat. That way there would be real *Shabbat Shalom* — real peace in the family, going into Shabbat.

Nathan looked out the window. It was snowing lightly. He considered going outside to play, but after a moment decided it was probably too cold. The television looked more inviting. Besides playing soccer, television was the thing Nathan liked best in the world.

He ran into the kitchen, quickly put together a sandwich, then went back to the den. With the sandwich in one hand, and the remote control in the other, he hurled himself onto the couch.

Nathan switched on the television. He wondered to himself where that channel was — the one with all those old TV shows. He really liked those old shows. Even when his parents told him that they had watched the same shows when they were kids, he still liked them. Usually, if his parents enjoyed something, he would decide it was old-fashioned and that he didn't like it. His parents would tell him he was just being *davka.* When he asked what davka meant, they said it was the same as being "contrary." When he asked what "contrary" meant, they told him to look it up in the dictionary.

But he liked those old TV shows anyway, even if his parents had also liked them. There was the one about the seven people shipwrecked on an island. And there was the comedy about Lucy and Ricky Ricardo and their two best friends, Fred and Ethel Mertz. But the ones he liked best were the ones where the people had magical powers. There was one show about a witch who wiggled her nose. Every time Nathan tried to twitch his nose, his little brother would copy him (but his brother's little fingers would usually slide from being *on* his nose to being *in* his nose!). And there was another show about an astronaut and a genie in a bikini. The witch and the genie were both really pretty.

Nathan ate his sandwich, and changed channels again. He began to imagine how neat it would be to have magical powers, or to have a genie to fulfill his every command. Getting his sister to be unable to enter the bathroom would be the first thing on his list. Learning his Bar Mitzvah stuff would be next.

Nathan suddenly remembered that he had promised his father he would practice his Torah reading. His Bar Mitzvah was still almost a year away, but the Rabbi kept telling him not to leave it all to the last minute. The big day would sneak up on him, the Rabbi assured him, sooner than he expected. His father would tell him the same thing. Nathan was convinced that his father and the Rabbi were plotting together — how else could they keep coming up with exactly the same lines?

Not that Nathan really minded having to learn how to chant the blessings, and everything else. True, some days he resented it, but his sister always told him he would feel glad when he finally became a Bar Mitzvah. If only it wouldn't cut into his soccer practice so much.

The other guys on the team didn't really understand. When he tried to tell them about a Bar Mitzvah, they just stared at him as though he were from another planet. Nathan thought about a show he had seen on that channel with old movies. Aliens land on earth. Everyone is staring at them as they walk through the streets of New York. No one knows what to say to them. That's how Nathan felt watching his teammates stare at him with blank expressions. Bar Mitzvah? Was that a ritual from another planet? That's what they must be thinking, he reasoned.

Oh, well, he had promised his father he would practice his Torah reading, and a promise was a promise. Now, where had he put it? Oh, yeah, it was lying right there on the table, next to the couch, almost within reach. As he stretched out his arm to get it, Nathan rolled off the couch, and fell flat on the hard floor. Ouch! As he sat up, he knocked his head on the coffee table. Ouch! Rubbing his head, he recalled something his father had once said: "*Shwer zu sein a Yid — It's hard to be a Jew.*" Sometimes, his dad really got it right.

Nathan settled back onto the couch with his Torah reading. Some days it seemed easy enough. Other days, however, he would read maybe two verses, and his eyelids would start to grow heavy. The more he tried to read, the drowsier he became. The drowsier he became, the more the Hebrew letters began to dance and float before his eyes.

It happened to be one of those drowsy days. The letters began to float off the page. They hovered around Nathan's head. Then Nathan fell into a deep sleep. And he began to dream.

As Nathan dreamed, the falling snow outside began to pile up in great drifts. Suddenly, it was as if he were outside, digging in the snow. He didn't know why he was outside in the snow. And he certainly did not understand why he was on his hands and knees digging, especially when there was a nice, new snow shovel hanging in the garage.

Nathan stood up, and went to the garage, slipping and sliding along the way. He picked up the shovel, and began clearing the snow from the driveway. Now he knew for sure that he was only dreaming. Only in a dream would he shovel snow without his parents telling him to. Shoveling the driveway was his chore. His little brother was too small. His older sister usually made up some excuse about having too much homework and a test the next day. Nathan knew that if he had ever made the same excuse, no one would have ever believed him.

Nathan used to love the snow when he was his brother's age, before it became his job to shovel it. Snowball fights, and sledding down the hill in the park, were great fun. Even better, was building snow forts and snowmen.

He remembered one time especially well. All the other kids on the street were out building snowmen, and snowladies, and snowanimals. Nathan and his sister wanted to make something different. Their parents suggested that they make something Jewish.

"Like what?" they asked.

"Well, what about whitefish?" Dad chuckled, the way he usually did when he thought he had said something funny. But Nathan didn't really get the joke.

"I hate fish," was all his sister could say.

"Well, then, what about snowbagels?" Mom offered.

"Yeah," Nathan and his sister agreed. "Snowbagels."

So they made snowbagels. Some of them were just plain, with a nice hole in the middle. Some of them they covered with bits of gravel and pretended they were poppy seed bagels. With others, they put a couple of sheets of pink plastic between two layers of snow. They pretended they were snowbagels with lox. All of their friends came 'round to admire their expert work. Chris, their ten-year-old neighbor, didn't know what a bagel was.

"Why are you making tires?" he asked, innocently.

"They're bagels, Chris," Nathan told him. "That's Jewish holy bread," he added, starting to laugh.

"Very holy bread," his sister said, trying not to giggle.

"Oh," Chris answered, not wanting to say anything bad about holy bread.

As Nathan continued to shovel, something flew up into the air. Nathan dropped the shovel, and went over to see what the object was. "How did these get here?" he said out loud. He had uncovered his spiked soccer shoes.

The shoes were all wet and covered in mud. Bad news — these were his only soccer shoes, and his mother would be angry with him. She would probably go into one of her speeches about how expensive they were, and how he needed to be more responsible, and take better care of his things. Nathan groaned to himself just thinking about it. Then he brightened as he realized that, by next spring, the shoes probably wouldn't fit him anymore, anyway.

Just the same, he decided he'd better try to clean them up a bit. He returned the snow shovel to the garage and picked up an old rag. First he cleaned one shoe. Not so bad; the mud came off easily enough. Then he tried to clean the other shoe. That proved more difficult. The mud was caked on, and refused to come off the shoe without a struggle. He rubbed. He rubbed harder. He rubbed his hardest.

Whew, these things really stink, he thought to himself. No wonder his sister always pretended to throw up when he would take off his shoes and wiggle his feet in her face as she lay watching TV.

And then, something strange happened.

Smoke began to pour out from the shoe. Just a little, at first. Then more. Then a steady stream of smoke, which turned into a great, dense cloud. He remembered from Scouts that rubbing two sticks together long enough could start a fire. Something about friction.

"Wow!" Nathan thought to himself. "I've been rubbing this shoe so hard that it's caught on fire!" He quickly dropped the shoe to the ground.

A funnel-cloud of smoke continued streaming from the shoe. At first, it was grey-white. Then, it began to turn bright green, then yellow, then violet-purple, then rosy-pink, then Coke-can red, then a sort of orange color, which reminded him of the color of Mrs. Lipsky's hair.

And then, the smoke turned into Mrs. Lipsky herself. At least, it looked like Mrs. Lipsky. She was dressed differently — more like the harem dancers in the pictures from the book his mother used to read to him, *1001 Arabian Nights*, or kinda like the ladies in that movie *Aladdin*, or maybe a little bit like Wonder Woman in the comic books — but it was definitely Mrs. Lipsky.

"Hey, Mrs. Lipsky. What are you doing here during the Winter vacation? Shouldn't you be getting stuff ready for your kids for Hanukkah or somethin'?" Nathan felt a little dazed, but thought he should say something that would impress her with how much he knew about his religion. "Hey, you're dressed pretty funny. It's too soon for Purim."

"Mrs. *Who*?" the lady asked. "Oh, Master Nathan, I know not who this Mrs. Lipsky might be, to whom thou referrest. But if thou wishest to call me by that name, so be it. Whatsoever givest thou pleasure, my Master, is my greatest desire!"

"Huh?" replied Nathan. "You sure talk funny."

"Hey, kiddo. Like I can talk any ol' way you want. If you want me to talk like this, that's cool with me. Like, okay, Master?"

"Sure," Nathan began to recover. "But who *are* you? *What* are you?"

"I'm the Genie of the Gym Shoe. And I've been trapped inside that smelly thing for who knows how long. Three thousand years maybe. If you had ever bothered to clean those shoes like your mother always told you, I would have been out of there long ago.

"By the way, my real name's Joanie." She shook Nathan's hand. "You released me from my imprisonment, so that makes you my master. And that means you get three wishes."

"They're soccer shoes, not gym shoes. And what were you doing inside my soccer shoe in the first place?" asked Nathan, not relating to what the genie had first said.

"Soccer, schmoccer. So many questions," she

began. "That nogoodnick, Pharoah, put me in there to punish me, about thirty centuries ago. And then another fellow named Moses took me with him when he led his people out of Egypt. Nice fellow, that Moses. Now, what about those three wishes?" Joanie waited for Nathan's answer.

Nathan realized that the genie meant what she said. He was so overwhelmed, he didn't know what to ask for.

"Well, I'm feeling pretty hungry after shoveling all that snow and rubbing those shoes. I wish I had something to eat," Nathan replied.

"Honey, the last guy who said that lost his birthright to his younger brother. You sure you want to waste a wish on something like that?" Joanie the Genie asked. "Tell you what, sweetie. I'm a little hungry myself. I've been inside that shoe for quite a long time. How 'bout we order out for a pizza? You know any place around here that delivers? By the way, I only eat kosher. Learned that from Moses himself." Joanie pulled a cellular phone out from her pink pantaloons.

"A genie with a cellular phone. Cool!" Nathan gave her the phone number.

"Veggie or cheese?" Joanie the Genie asked.

Nathan said that cheese and tomato would be just fine. "Now, tell me again about those three wishes."

Joanie explained that Nathan could make any three wishes that his heart desired. Her job was to make them come true. But he had to make it quick. His mother would be back before too long. He also might wake up and the dream would be over. And, besides, she didn't do wishes after sundown on Friday, since it would be Shabbat.

"Wow, any three wishes...."

"But no windows. I don't do windows," Joanie the Genie chuckled. It reminded him of the way his father would chuckle whenever he made a joke which Nathan did not quite understand. "But think about it carefully," the genie cautioned. "You don't want to have any regrets.

"Oh, and, by the way, don't try to pull any funny business. You're not allowed to make two wishes and then make a third wish for three more wishes. It's against union rules. The last guy who tried it — well, you don't want to know. All the genies went on strike for 1001 nights. Some fellow named Aladdin tried to cross the picket line and — well, let's just say we really pulled the rug out from under him. So, — three wishes and only three wishes. Now, what's it gonna be?"

"Wow, any three wishes..." Nathan repeated.

"So, nu? That pizza's going to be here, soon." Joanie the Genie sounded impatient as she tried to move things along. "Why don't you just tell me all three wishes together, and I'll take care of them in the blink of an eye."

Nathan drew a deep breath as he began. "OK, here goes. I wish... I wish that I didn't have to make Shabbat every week with my family. That way I could be like the other kids and just play soccer. That's my first wish. And I wish I didn't have to go to Hebrew School, and Religious School, and study so much for a Bar Mitzvah. That's my second wish. And I'd like to be able to celebrate Christmas. That's my third wish. Yeah, that's what I wish for. How's that?"

The Genie of the Gym Shoe looked startled. "I had no idea you felt so ambivalent about being Jewish!"

"What's that mean? Ambivalent?" Nathan looked puzzled.

"A-M-B-I-V-A-L-E-N-T. Look it up in the dictionary."

"You sound like my parents."

Joanie snapped her fingers and she was suddenly holding a dictionary. She snapped her fingers again. This time a remote control gizmo appeared. She handed Nathan the remote control. "Page 23," she said.

Nathan punched in the number 23 and the pages turned automatically.

"'*Ambivalent: Feelings of conflict about something. Mixed feelings.*' Yeah, I guess that's me. I mean,

I like being Jewish most of the time. But, sometimes, I wish I could be just like everybody else. And I wish I could play soccer whenever I want — even on Friday nights or instead of studying for my Bar Mitzvah."

Joanie the Genie looked hard at Nathan. "Are you sure you understand what it is you're wishing for? Like, maybe you want to think about it for a little while? I mean, the pizza's not here yet."

"But you were in a pretty big hurry a minute ago. No, I'm sure. Those are my three wishes. That's what I want." Once Nathan had made up his mind about something, he did not change it easily. His parents had told him that was another meaning for *davka* — stubborn.

"J'll tell you what, sweetie. You seem like a nice kid. I liked you as soon as I met you. I think that before I grant you your three wishes, maybe we should take a moment to assess them. How 'bout I show you how those three wishes will affect you, and then you can decide if that's what you'd really like to wish for, okay?"

Joanie snapped her fingers and a television suddenly appeared beside Nathan. "Do you ever watch TV, by any chance?" Before he could answer, she popped in a video. "Great invention, these videos. If Moses could have shown Pharoah what would happen, the old king would have avoided — like the plague — starting up with Moses. There'd be a lot more frogs around, too."

Joanie pressed the remote control. "Do you mind if I fast forward through the previews of coming attractions? It'll save us some time, and you still have a lot of snow to shovel after we're finished."

Nathan watched the screen as the video began. First the credits rolled across: "Truth and Covenant Productions...in cooperation with Blue Genies and Levis Enterprises, and (a picture of a giant beetle roaring), The Beetle Jews Company, present: *To Redo a Jew*, Directed by Joanie the Gym Shoe Genie, and starring: (big bold letters) NATHAN the ambivalent adolescent. Produced at Look It Up In the Dictionary Studios, and co-starring, Nathan's mom, dad, older sister, and younger brother, with cameo appearances by...."

The video continued to roll, but Nathan's eyes were already growing heavy. How strange he felt. It was as if he were living inside those old television shows he enjoyed watching on that one particular channel.

Nathan looked around him. The weather sure seemed warm for December. Only moments ago it had been snowing. Now the sun was blazing and the air felt moist. All about him, the landscape was lush and green. Giant coconut palms towered above him. Leafy plants extended as far as his eyes could see. He suddenly noticed that he was no longer wearing his heavy coat, ear muffs, or woolen gloves. Instead, he was wearing his soccer uniform and shoes.

Hearing voices not far away, he began to walk in their direction. He was struck by all the brightly colored, sweet-smelling flowers in shades of red, and pink, and yellow. As he walked along, he passed a lagoon of calm and peaceful waters. He noticed at one edge of the pool a boat, badly damaged, with a large hole in its side. Written on the side of the vessel were the words, "*S.S. Minnow.*" It sounded somehow familiar to Nathan.

He continued walking, the distant voices growing nearer. As he looked up towards the sun, trying to decide in which direction he was going, he noticed an especially tall palm tree with a huge cluster of coconuts hanging down. But, wait! They weren't coconuts. They were soccer balls! This was definitely Nathan's idea of paradise.

The voices were much closer now. He reached a clearing and peered from behind a shrub. There were several huts built of bamboo, each with a thatched roof. There were also two goal posts made of bamboo. He saw seven people — three women and four men.

One woman was tall, with auburn hair, and wearing a long evening gown. One woman was older, with silver-red hair, and wearing an elegant suit. The third was young, dark-haired with two braids, and wearing blue jeans.

The men were an equally odd assortment. The oldest one was wearing a navy blue blazer and a turtleneck. Another one had a large potbelly and wore a skipper's cap. He heard them refer to the third one as "Professor." The last of the seven was thin, with a silly grin, and wearing a white cap and bell-bottomed trousers.

He heard one of them say, "Okay, let's divide up teams. Mr. Howell, Ginger, and the Professor on one team. Mrs. Howell, the Skipper, and Mary Ann on the other team. And who wants Gilligan?"

Could it really be that Nathan was on...?

"That's right, lovey," a voice called down from a thatched roof. "You're on *Gilligan's Island*." Nathan looked up and saw Joanie the Genie wink at him. "And you're just in time for a soccer match."

The Skipper suddenly saw Nathan rustling in the bushes. "Hey, gang! Look who I found. An eighth. Now we can have even teams of four. After all these years on this island. What's your name, little buddy? Do you play soccer?"

"Nathan, sir. And, yes, I love soccer."

"Hey, Skipper! I thought I was your little buddy," Gilligan said, looking hurt.

"You're also my little buddy, Little Buddy. But we want Nathan to feel welcomed. Okay, Nate, little buddy; can you play goalie?"

"You betcha."

"Then you're on the Professor's team. Gilligan, Little Buddy, you'll play on our side."

The video began to speed ahead. Day after day, the gang on Gilligan's Island played soccer. Day in and day out. Usually Gilligan would mess up some play, and the Skipper would yell at him. Then they would all make-up. Mr. Howell would try to get everyone to bet on the games. The Professor would devise new strategies. Ginger Grant would trip over her evening gown and pout. Mrs. Howell could never really understand the rules of the game, and Mary Ann was always a good sport about everything. Meanwhile, Nathan grew tanned and fit and happy being the star player.

Sometimes they changed teams, but otherwise each day was much the same as the one before. Over and over again, day in and day out. And then the gang on Gilligan's Island went into re-runs, and syndication, and the whole routine continued without interruption.

Once, Nathan asked the gang what day it was. "What difference does it make?" the Skipper replied.

"On a tropical island, everyday is the same. Everyday is easy. Everyday is uneventful."

"But doesn't the same thing get to you after a while?" Nathan asked. "When do you ever tell each other that you care about each other? When do you ever take a break from soccer or take a break from trying to get rescued from this island? Don't you have a day that's different, like Shabbat?"

The gang looked puzzled. These questions had never occurred to them before. So Nathan tried to explain about Shabbat. He told them it was about thanking God for the beauty of Creation and for a different kind of rescue — the rescue from physical slavery in Egypt. The rescue from sameness.

Then, he decided to show them how to make Shabbat.

They set up a table one afternoon, and covered it with flowers. They swept the huts clean, and gathered delicious foods for dinner. Then they sat around the table. Nathan taught them about the blessings for the candles, and for the Kiddush wine, and for washing the hands, and for the bread. He taught Mr. Howell about a husband's special song for his wife. He taught the Skipper and Gilligan about a father's blessing for his children.

As they ate dinner, they sang the songs he had taught them. Nathan looked around the table. Everyone there had been so nice to him. But it wasn't the same kind of Shabbat as he remembered at home. He looked at the faces around the table. They gradually blurred and became the faces he knew and loved most.

There was his mother, closing her eyes and blessing the candles. There was his father, blessing him, and his sister, and his brother; giving them each a kiss on the forehead. His father would turn to his mother and sing her the "Woman of Valor" song, and kiss her, too. They would then raise their silver Kiddush goblets and sing the blessing over wine, together. And then his little brother, waiting impatiently for his special moment, would remove the cover from the two loaves of *challah* like a matador, and look up with a grin.

Nathan cried. Then he laughed as he discovered how much it all meant to him, and how very much he missed it. Missed the warmth, and peace, and family closeness. Missed the break from his old weekly routine of school, and homework, and family squabbles, and even from his after school routine — soccer. He suddenly realized that the only thing which deserved to go into re-runs was the Shabbat.

"Joanie!" he called out. "I've changed my mind!"

"Thought you might," Joanie called down from the thatched roof. "Ready to check out Wish Number Two?"

"Ready any time you are," Nathan called back.

Suddenly a giant coconut — or was it a soccer ball? — dropped from the palm tree under which Nathan stood. Bonk! It fell squarely on Nathan's head. His eyes closed, and....

When Nathan awoke and looked around him, there were no more palm trees nor any lush tropical greenery. In fact, everything was black, and white, and grey. It looked like someone's apartment. He decided to have a little peek around. He was in the living room. There was a fireplace and a window with a piano in front of it. The furniture reminded him of his grandmother's. (His mother had always called it 1950's modern.) He stuck his head behind one door. There was a small kitchen with a back door leading to a fire escape and shutters overlooking the living room. The other side of the living room led to a bedroom with twin beds. That was about all there was to it.

As Nathan tried to figure out where he was, the back door opened. A lady walked in wearing a housedress and apron, her hair in curlers. She was blonde, a little bit heavy, which his father called *zaftik*, and perhaps fifteen years older than his own mother. She poured a cup of coffee, helped herself to a sweet roll, and, with her mouth full, said, "Morning, Lucy. What did you do to your hair? Yesterday it was red."

Nathan looked around and blinked. "Are you talking to me? My name isn't Lucy. It's Nathan."

"Of course I'm talking to you, Lucy. Don't you recognize me? It's Ethel. Oh, you poor little thing. I knew this would happen one day. You've been scheming to get into Ricky's act for so long that you've finally lost it. You don't even know who you are anymore. By the way, I liked your hair better when it was red."

Nathan decided it was best to go along with Ethel and just pretend to be Lucy. (Dreams really can be very weird things!)

"So what's new with you, Ethel?"

"Not much," she said, still chewing. "Fred tells me that Ricky is putting together a new show down at the club. Some kind of Jewish Bar Mitzvah thing. They're having auditions all this week. Oops, Fred told me not to say anything about it. Ricky doesn't want you trying to get into the act."

"Ricky's doing a new show down at the club? A Jewish Bar Mitzvah? I could do that. I'd be perfect for the part. He's always trying to keep me from getting into show business. That Cuban ham is afraid I'll upstage him. Well, I'll show him. This will be the first Bar Mitzvah to have not just one, but two hams."

"Lucy, I hate it when you get that look in your eyes."

"Ethel, I have a plan. Will you help me?"

The plan was brilliant, and simple, and completely kookie. Lucy — or, rather, Nathan — would hire a tutor. By day, the tutor would secretly teach her everything a person needed to know about being a Jew: the prayers and blessings, the holidays, the laws of *kashrut* and the meaning of the *mitzvot*, the Bible, the Talmud, the Midrash, the history of Israel, how to read Hebrew, and how to chant from the Torah and the Haftorah.

It was a lot to learn in a single, half-hour episode. But Lucy was convinced it could be done. It couldn't possibly be any harder than working in a chocolate factory, or climbing the Empire State Building dressed as a martian, or stealing John Wayne's footprints from a Hollywood street. Besides, if Jewish kids have been learning all this stuff for hundreds and thousands of years, Lucy was sure she could, too.

Finally, on the opening night of the big show, Lucy would dress up as a boy. She would sneak into Ricky's nightclub. No one would notice her. Then, at just the right moment, while Ricky's orchestra sang the *Shema* to the tune of *BaBaLoo*, she would leap onto the stage. She would take off her disguise, and show him she could perform a Bar Mitzvah.

The video began to speed ahead. Every day and every night, Lucy — or rather Nathan — would study the holy books, and read, and practice Hebrew. Soon, the big night arrived. Everything went as planned. Ricky's nightclub was packed with people. They had all heard about the new show called "Havana Gilah." As the lights dimmed and the conga drums began to pound out a song, Lucy leaped onto the stage, right into the spotlight. She was ready. She was ready to sing the prayers. Ready to chant the Torah and Haftorah. Ready to give a *devar Torah* — a speech explaining her Torah portion and teaching a lesson. She looked out over the crowd. There were so many people. And then she saw the faces of her family — Nathan's family, really. There were Nathan's mother and father, his older sister, and younger brother. Even his grandparents were there. She looked over to where Ethel had been sitting. But Ethel was no longer there. How very odd. In her place, Lucy/Nathan saw Joanie the Genie. She smiled at him. Then she winked.

Nathan opened his mouth to begin. He was eager to show all he had learned about being a Jew. His family watched proudly. They all looked at him, expectantly. But when he opened his mouth, the words would not come out. He tried again. Still nothing happened. In fact, he had gone completely blank. All his knowledge seemed to vanish.

He did not understand. He didn't feel nervous, so it could not be stage fright. But he was beginning to feel very embarrassed. It was suddenly as though he knew nothing about the Torah or about being a Jew.

Just then Ricky came on stage. He looked angry. "Lucy, you got some 'splaining to do!" Then he started yelling in Spanish.

All Nathan could do was to start crying. "But I'm not Lucy. I'm Nathan," he protested. And then he looked across the room and shouted, "Joanie the Genie, you got some 'splaining to do!"

Everyone in the room vanished, except for Nathan and Joanie. Joanie put her arm around his shoulder and said, "You wished that you didn't have to go to Religious School, and to Hebrew School, and to Bar Mitzvah lessons. This is what would happen if you got your wish. You wouldn't know how to be Jewish. You wouldn't know what it means to be Jewish. You wouldn't be able to do anything Jewish. Worst of all, you wouldn't be able to teach your children about being Jewish or to explain it to anyone else.

"Nathan, my young friend, you can say to people that you're proud to be a Jew. But if you don't learn about it, how can you know what it is that you're proud of? And if you don't spend the time and effort to learn about it, how proud can you really be? Remember what your father told you? '*Shwer zu sein a Yid — It's hard to be a Jew.*' I guess he meant that it takes a lot of work."

Nathan replied thoughtfully, "Maybe I've been a little too davka for my own good. I want to feel and know what it is to be a Jew."

"Nathan, I couldn't have 'splained it any better than that. Are you ready to check out Wish Number Three?"

"Ready any time you are." Nathan saw Joanie take out a silver pointer used to read the Torah. She pointed it at him and wiggled her nose. It was all he remembered as he closed his eyes.

When he next opened his eyes, Nathan saw that his world had returned to living color. He felt a little tired after visiting the gang on Gilligan's Island. He felt a little confused after spending time with the Ricardos and the Mertzs.

Looking around him, he now felt bewitched. It bothered and bewildered him. He was standing in someone's home. It was a very nice home. He wandered through the living and dining rooms, the kitchen, and the study. It was all neat as a pin, except that in the study there were some drawings and sketches spread out over the desk. Nathan took a closer look at them. They all said, "Ad campaign for McMann and Tate."

Wandering back out into the living room, he saw someone coming down the stairs. She was slim, and blonde, and very pretty. She smiled warmly as she greeted him.

"Hello, Nathan. I'm Samantha Stevens. I've been expecting you. Make yourself at home. My husband, Darren, isn't here or he would probably offer you a dry martini. It's the first thing he usually does. But you look a little young for martinis to me."

"How do you know my name?"

"Joanie and I are old friends. We work out together at the same health club. It takes a lot of exercise to keep her blink and my twitch in good shape. We've been thinking about producing a video called 'Crones of Steel.' Joanie tells me you've been wishing to have Christmas. Is that true?"

Nathan saw his opportunity. "Yes, yes. Please. Ever since I was little, I've wanted it. Can you do it, Sam?"

"Easiest thing in the world. The only problem is that I promised Darren there would be no witchcraft in this house." She giggled. "Not that it's ever stopped me. You know, I could probably use a little help... MOTHER!"

Nathan looked up at the ceiling and saw a lady suspended in mid-air. She had red hair, lots of eye make-up, and wore a flowing gown of green and purple. Funny, too; she looked an awful lot like his teacher, Miss Henderson.

"Nathan, I want you to meet my mother, Endora. Mother, this is Nathan."

"Nice to meet you, Newton."

"Nathan, Mother. Not Newton," Samantha corrected.

"Nathan, Newton. These mortals are all *Nudniks*," Endora yawned. "Now, why have you interrupted me? I was dining with a perfectly delightful *dybbuk* I used to date before I met your father. This better be important."

"It is, Mother. Nathan is Jewish, but he's been wishing he could have Christmas. I thought you and I could help him out," Samantha explained, with a twinkle in her eye.

"Christmas, eh? Are you sure that's what you desire, Neville?" Endora smiled in a way that made him uneasy.

"It's *Nathan*, Mother. Not Neville. And we're doing this as a favor for a friend of mine."

"Oh, all right. Let's get on with it, so I can get back to my darling little dybbuk before he loses interest and goes chasing after some other demon twenty centuries younger than myself."

Endora waved her arm and muttered some kind of incantation. In an instant Nathan heard reindeer paws and bells on the roof. He looked at the fireplace, and, lo, coming down the chimney was good ol' Santa Claus.

Samantha called to her mother. "Show off! It's not fair that you should have all the fun." She wiggled her nose. A tall evergreen tree suddenly appeared in a corner of the living room. Another twitch, and the tree was ablaze with twinkling lights and ornaments. One more twitch, and the entire room was filled with holiday decorations.

"Child's play, Samantha." Endora waved her other arm in a grand sweeping gesture. Beautifully wrapped gifts appeared under the tree. A crew of elves sat working in another corner of the room. A dozen people, singing carols, stood in a third corner.

Samantha twitched her nose one more time. The dining room table was immediately filled with sweets and all types of delicious foods. "And now, a few finishing touches," she announced. A snap of her fingers and snow began to collect on the window panes. Candles appeared in the windows. Nathan heard more sleigh bells outside. He also heard the doorbell ring. In walked more people: Larry Tate, Mr. and Mrs. Kravitz, Aunt Clara, Serena, Dr. Bombay, and three bewildered kings.

"Okay, Nathan. Time to open all the presents." Samantha gave him a gentle push towards the tree. Nathan needed no further urging. He rushed to the tree and began tearing off the gift wrap, and opening up all the boxes. And then....

It was over. In about ten minutes, it was all over.

"Is that it?" Nathan looked up at Samantha, wistfully.

"That's it until next year."

"Oh," Nathan replied weakly. "It doesn't last very long, or seem to mean very much. I thought it would seem more important than this. Isn't Christmas a religious holiday?"

"For many people it is. And for them it does mean something more. For them it's a sacred season, a special day to be spent in the warmth of family and friends. But you're Jewish, Nathan. So it would not have the same religious meaning to you. I'm afraid that the only things you see are the gifts and pretty decorations. And that part is over, very quickly." Samantha waited to see what Nathan would do.

"This is getting too emotional for me. I'm outta here. Farewell, Nolan." And with a wave of her arms, Endora vanished.

Nathan felt a little disappointed. Christmas just wasn't at all what he expected. "You know, between those elves and those carolers, it's getting a little noisy and crowded in here. I'm not sure I really belong. Can we go somewhere a little quieter?"

Samantha led him into the study. Nathan began to look at all the drawings and sketches at which he had only glanced earlier. "It's an advertising campaign that Darren has been working on," Sam explained.

Nathan studied the drawings more closely. One said, *Rosh Hashanah — A Good and Sweet Year*. There was a picture of a *shofar* and apples with honey. Another said, *Yom Kippur — May You Be Sealed for Good in the Book of Life*. There was a picture of people dressed in white, their heads bowed in prayer. A third sketch said, *Sukkot — Season of Our Joy*. There were illustrations of a family decorating a *sukkah* and having dinner beneath the stars. The next drawing had a picture of people dancing with a Torah scroll. It read *Simchat Torah*.

There were at least a half-dozen additional pictures spread around the room. One said, *Hanukkah — The Weak Against The Strong*. Another said, *Purim — The Few Against The Many* and depicted people in costumes making lots of noise whenever they heard the name of *Haman*. There was one labeled *Tu b'Shevat — New Year of Trees* with people planting trees and eating fruits. There was a small one called *Lag b'Omer* showing a big bonfire with children playing with bows and arrows. And there were two very big cards. The first one said, *Passover* and showed a large family gathered around a table, reading from the *Hagaddah* and eating all kinds of foods while children searched for the hidden *afiko-*

men. The second one said, *Shavuot — The Ten Commandments Are Born* and had pictures of the Torah and the Ten Commandments, as well as delicious cheesecakes and blintzes.

And then Nathan saw the biggest drawing board of all. It was called *Shabbat.* It showed a picture of a family gathered around a table, looking very happy. The amazing thing was that the faces looked an awful lot like those of his own family.

As Nathan examined all the drawings, Samantha interrupted his thoughts. "Your people have so many wonderful holidays. And they give meaning to your life throughout the year. Would you really be willing to trade them in for Christmas?"

"I guess not," Nathan answered, truthfully.

"And if you really celebrated all Hanukkah the way you should, do you think you would really want to have Christmas so badly?"

"I guess not," Nathan repeated.

"You know what I think?" Samantha continued. "I think that when you put all your Jewish holidays together, even the sad or serious ones, you have more magic in your life than anything I could conjure up. That's what I think."

"That's what I think, too," Nathan agreed.

The two of them walked back out to the living room. Everyone was gone now, and the room was cluttered with the shredded remains of gift wrapping.

"Maybe Judaism has given me the best gift of all," said Nathan.

Samantha twitched approvingly, one last time, and the lights went out.

Nathan looked around and saw that he was, once again, standing in his own driveway. He was wearing his heavy coat, his ear muffs, and his woolen gloves. It was still snowing, and Nathan shivered. Joanie the Genie was standing beside him, and the video in the TV was drawing to a close. The final words, "Filmed in MannaVision," rolled past and Nathan looked at Joanie.

"By the way, I've been meaning to ask," Nathan said, "aren't you cold? How can you genies dress like that in this weather?"

"It's very simple, *boychik*. I'm only a figment of your imagination. Figments don't get cold. Any more questions?"

"Can I still change my mind about those three wishes? I'm not so sure they were very wise wishes, after all. I've decided that it's a pretty good thing to be Jewish. I like it, and wouldn't want to be anything else. Even though it means being different. Even though it means not playing soccer all the time. Even though it means having to study. Yeah, even though it means not having Christmas.

"But, I still want my three wishes? What should I wish for?" He thought about sending his sister to Gilligan's Island. He wondered how his little brother would sound with a Spanish accent.

"Maybe after you think about it some more you can call me back," Joanie said. "I'll give you an IOU for those three wishes. All you have to do is rub that gym shoe."

"It's a soccer shoe, not a gym shoe."

"Soccer, schmoccer," Joanie smiled. "Just rub the shoe. You may outgrow it by next spring, but you'll never outgrow wishing and dreaming. Of course, by next spring you may realize that you don't need a genie to make your wishes come true. You already have everything you need. Your family. Your teachers. Your education. Your Jewish traditions."

"I wouldn't bet on it," Nathan told her.

"Listen, little buddy. It's almost Shabbat and I still have a few things to do. I really need to get going." She gave him a wink and said, "*Shabbat Shalom. I'll see you at your Bar Mitzvah. I'll be sitting next to Miss Henderson. I'll be the short zaftik one.*" And with that, she was gone.

Nathan heard the back door open as his mother, sister, and little brother returned home. Rolling over, he yawned, stretched, and rubbed his eyes. He was no longer home, alone. His mother walked in carrying shopping bags. His sister was holding some flowers. His little brother proudly displayed a *challah*. Nathan jumped off the couch to help them.

His mother glanced around the room. *I Dream of Jeannie* was playing on the TV. A half-eaten sandwich was on the table.

"Hi, honey. Enjoying the first day of Winter vacation? I don't suppose you've done any work on your assignments?" She already knew the answer.

As if on cue, the telephone rang. It was the Rabbi, reminding Nathan of his Bar Mitzvah lesson the following Monday. As Nathan hung up, the phone rang again. This time it was Miss Henderson.

"Nathan, I just wanted to remind you that I still expect that makeup assignment to be on my desk as soon as you come back from Winter vacation. Don't fritter away all your time watching television."

"Tell me again. What was I supposed to be writing about?" Nathan replied weakly.

"A philosopher named Gottfried Lessing. And a story he wrote entitled *Nathan the Wise*. Very famous. It's about religious tolerance, and why we should appreciate our own traditions."

"Oh yeah, right. I remember now."

"Five pages long. Have a nice vacation."

"Yeah, right." Nathan hung up.

The phone rang once more. "Nathan? Hi, it's Dad. Don't forget to shovel the driveway. Is your mom there?"

Nathan handed the phone to his mother. Some vacation this was starting out to be. His Torah reading was waiting. And that school assignment about Nathan the Wise Guy, or something. And the driveway to shovel.

He thought about it for a moment and wished he had a genie to make all that work disappear. Then he brightened. "Would taking care of all my homework for winter recess count as three wishes?" he wondered out loud.

"What was that, dear?" his mother asked.

"Nothing, Mom," Nathan answered, noticing something sticking out from under the couch. "Nothing at all, Mom."

He smiled as he took out his soccer shoe from under the couch, and headed for his room.

Hannah's

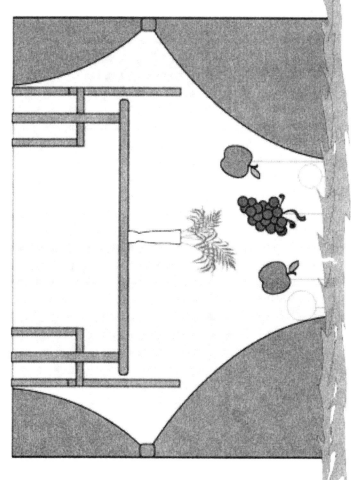

Sukkah

Mindy Aber Barad *is an attorney who has lived most of her life in Israel.*

While in college, Ms. Barad co-founded the Jewish Student Newspaper Hamakor *at Washington University in St. Louis.*

Her interests include law, the study of Torah, music, (she is an accomplished musician), midwifery, and early childhood psychology and development.

She and her husband live in Jerusalem with their four beautiful children, and a large dog.

In this story, a young girl learns that building a sukkah can have some very funny, and frustrating, consequences.

*O*ne week before Rosh Hashanah, the Jewish New Year, Mrs. Zelkin decided to take all the kids to the museum. "The museum" meant the Israel Museum, and taking all the kids was not an easy decision to make.

"Take me, take me!" each child shouted.

"I promise I'll behave, Mom," said Hannah, who was ten years old, and the eldest of the four children. "I'll help you."

"Yeah, I'll help too," said Boaz, a year younger.

"Me, too," said Jesse, the five-year-old.

"Me, twee," announced Eli, the three-year-old, raising three fingers into the air.

Eli and Jesse looked like twins. They had the same squeezable cheeks, blue eyes and blonde hair. The only difference between them was that Jesse was taller. And, sometimes, Eli didn't pronounce his words so well.

"Well, if you're all going to be helpful, then I'm sure we'll have a good time," Mrs. Zelkin answered.

Skip, their new puppy, began barking.

"Mom, Skip wants to come with us, too," Boaz said.

"Skip, twee," Eli told everyone, holding up fingers. Technically, Eli was right. Skip was only three months old.

"Sorry," said Mrs. Zelkin. "The museum is only for people. We'll be back soon."

That day, there was a special exhibit at the Jewish Museum about the Jews of Afghanistan. They started there first.

"Wow, look at all that good food," Jesse said. There was a display of trays filled with all kinds of dried fruits, sweets, and nuts.

"Look at the fabrics on the wall," Hannah said. There were beautifully woven fabrics, with different patterns. "They look like Persian carpets!"

"Persian!? This is Afghanistan, dummy," Boaz corrected her.

"No *dummies*, kids, please," said Mrs. Zelkin.

"But she said they're like Persian carpets, and this is Afghanistan," Boaz explained.

"*She* has a name," Hannah interrupted.

"Godzilla said they're like Persian...," Boaz countered.

"I'm not interested in your arguments, as long as there are no *dummies*. Besides, Persia and Afghanistan are close enough geographically that Hannah was not far off the mark."

Boaz and Hannah stared at one another.

"Where's Eli?" Mrs. Zelkin asked, suddenly whirling around to look for him.

"Eliiiii," Jesse called.

"Shh, not in the Museum!" Mrs. Zelkin said.

The children began running around the exhibit looking for their little lost brother.

"Here he is!" called Hannah. "He's sitting on a dummy!"

"Shh," Mrs. Zelkin reminded her.

"Here I'm am!" Eli whispered.

Sure enough, there was Eli, sitting on the lap of the mannequin dressed in Afghani wedding clothes, eating the goodies on a tray.

"Deese cakes are even harder than the ones Hannah made," complained Eli.

"Hey, how come Hannah can say dummy and I can't?" Boaz complained.

"Because I know when to use the word 'dummy,'" Hannah said, in her own defense.

"See! She said it again," insisted Boaz. "Takes one to know one," he added.

"Quiet!" shouted Mrs. Zelkin. Then, seeing heads of other visitors turned to her, she repeated in a whisper, "Quiet."

"Mom, look at these fabrics over here!" Hannah pointed, changing the subject. "They're even nicer than the other ones," Hannah said, ignoring her youngest brother now that he was found.

"All you can talk about is fabric, fabric, all the time," Boaz grumbled.

"Shh," Mrs. Zelkin said. "Eli come out of there. You know you're not supposed to run away from us. This is a museum exhibit, dear. You must never touch, and certainly never climb on anything."

Pity I left the leash on the dog, she thought. I could use it now. She realized she was showing the first signs of exasperation.

Mrs. Zelkin looked at Hannah and Boaz, "And I thought you older two were going to help. From now on, the hand-holding rule is in effect. Hannah, you get Eli. Boaz, you get Jesse. Jesse? Now where did he wander off to?"

Everyone fanned out. Jesse was found nearby, examining some Afghani clothes that were hanging on clotheslines.

"They have laundry here, Mom," he said, "but I think someone stole all their underpants and socks!"

"They walked around barefoot a lot in those days, didn't they, Mom?" Hannah said, trying to sound grown-up.

"Didn't they have their own feet?" Jesse asked, innocently.

Hannah and Boaz laughed.

Eli announced that he was afraid of the bear.

Mrs. Zelkin wasn't quite sure if Jesse was pulling *her* leg or not.

Having finished their Afghani adventure, they all proceeded to the Ethnography exhibit, because Hannah begged, pleading, "I want to compare the fabrics there with the ones we just saw."

"What! Fabrics again!?" Boaz exclaimed in a voice that was too loud.

"What!? I have to shush you again!?" Mrs. Zelkin said. Boaz got the message.

"Hannah, dear, you take Eli and look at fabrics. I'll take these two guys and look at other things."

It's hard to explain what the Ethnography section of the Museum is, but if you ever go there, you understand. There are exhibits of clothing and utensils used by Jews from around the world. You can see their different tools, dishes, pots and pans, and furniture, too. The different ways of life are exhibited in glass cases.

One glass case enclosed a typical living room of Jews who lived in Germany 100 years ago. Another case displayed a typical kitchen from the same time period. Short films about the Jews of different countries were shown on television screens in the darkened corners of the Ethnography exhibit.

Hannah stopped beside the Moroccan room. She loved the look of all those rich bright colors, pillows on low benches, carpets covering the floor, and the walls, too. The colors didn't clash at all. They blended beautifully.

"Look," Eli said to her, "so many weddings." He was pointing to displays of mannequins dressed in various ethnic wedding finery. Each display was encased in glass, so Hannah didn't have to worry that Eli would find his way into a wedding party again!

"Mom, I want to see *the* beautiful room," Jesse

said, as they joined Hannah and Eli, a few minutes later.

"You mean the Rothschild Room," Mrs. Zelkin said.

"Hey, there's a sukkah!" Hannah exclaimed. They stopped at a wooden sukkah whose interior walls were beautifully painted.

"Isn't this just wonderful? But a little small for us," Hannah said.

"C'mon, we're going to see a much better room!" Jesse urged her on.

They continued past menorahs, Torah scrolls and other Judaica, until they arrived at the "Rothschild Room."

"Wow!" Jesse and Eli said together. "Tell us the story about the Rothschilds again," Jesse begged, referring to the famous Rothschild family.

So, Mrs. Zelkin began the story of the Rothschilds. In the 1700's, Amshel Rothschild sent each of his children off to a different city in Europe to expand the family fortune. The brothers communicated between cities by special messengers and carrier pigeons. They made their fortunes in banking and trade. Kings and emperors sometimes depended on the Rothschilds for information, via their special communications system. They also depended on the Rothschilds to finance their wars and other grandiose projects.

The Rothschilds were tremendously wealthy, and owned collections of fine art and other valuable things. They also gave a lot of charity. They sent money to Israel, even before it became a state, to build hospitals, schools, farms and to help the Jews of Israel get businesses started and live their lives in their own land. This was perhaps their most important contribution to the world.

"And this is the sitting room rebuilt from the house of the Rothschild brother who lived in Paris," Mrs. Zelkin said. Before them, roped off, was a tremendous room with a few couches and tables. The ceiling and walls were decorated in gold. Large paintings hung on the walls. Magnificent candlesticks stood on tables along the sides of the room. There was also a desk and some chairs.

"Just imagine, children, all this in only one room, and they had a whole house like this."

"Did they let their kids run around in this room?" Jesse asked.

"Did they *had* to be quiet?" Eli asked.

"Did they *have* to be quiet, you mean? I'm sure they had to be quiet. Their father was a very busy and important man," Mrs. Zelkin explained.

"Dad likes this room too, right, Mom?"

"Yes, children, he certainly does," Mrs. Zelkin said. "Probably because it's so quiet."

"Then why doesn't Dad work here?" Jesse

wanted to know. "That way, we could only bother him when we visit."

Mrs. Zelkin thought that her husband would probably appreciate their son's suggestion. Actually, she thought to herself, I wouldn't mind some quiet time here, myself.

It was time to go. They hurried back out the way they came, Mrs. Zelkin rushing to get home. As they passed the Impressionist paintings, Boaz said, "Wait, Mom, I always wanted to ask you about this painting." Boaz was standing in front of a painting by Magritte. The picture showed a huge boulder suspended in a blue and white sky. On top of the boulder was a large castle.

"I never figured out how the people get home in this picture, and how they keep from falling off. I don't understand it."

"Maybe no one's home," suggested Jesse.

"It's a Poly Pockets," Eli chimed in. He was collecting miniature houses called Poly Pockets.

"That's where God lives," Boaz said, joking.

"No wonder we don't see anyone," Eli added. "God is imbizzable."

"He's just joking," Hannah pointed out. "This just shows how everyone can make their own castle in the world, if they want to."

Mrs. Zelkin was impressed with Hannah's answer, but she didn't want to make the other children jealous.

"Well, maybe Magritte painted it this way just so that you would ask those questions."

"Like kids asking questions at the *Seder* table," Hannah suggested.

"Something like that," Mrs. Zelkin said, beaming.

"Let's keep going, children," she urged, pushing them on, past the Judaica section, past the Museum shop, up the stairs, and out the main entrance.

Eli and Jesse made their way to the fountain in front of the entrance. Water splashed down a narrow channel that seemed to invite children to play.

Boaz, Eli and Jesse made straight for the fountain.

Mrs. Zelkin called out to them, "Boys, don't even think of it!" She continued rushing the children to the exit.

Just before the exit, Eli pulled away from Hannah.

"Look, the horse wif the big tushy!" He rushed over to the Botero sculpture of a man riding on a horse. The fun element of the sculpture was that the horse was completely out of proportion, with a small head and a big back-end.

"Can I ride on it?" Jesse asked.

"No, of course not," Mrs. Zelkin explained, as

she did each time they came. "It's just to look at."

"Who wants to look at a big tushy?" Jesse asked. Eli raised his hand.

As they all climbed into the car, Boaz announced, "I'm hungry."

"Me, too," Jesse said, followed by Eli, his echo. "Me, too."

"Hannah, you haven't said 'Me, too' yet. Are you dreaming?" Mrs. Zelkin asked, laughing.

"About fabric!" Boaz teased.

"Yes, as a matter of fact, how did you know?" Hannah said.

"Genius," Boaz answered, shrugging his shoulders.

"I'm dreaming, too," Jesse announced, his eyes closed.

"About what?" his mother asked.

Jesse had just remembered that no one had answered his question, "What happened to the people's clothing?"

"What happened to the underpants?" Eli asked. "I know about the bears, but what about the underpants?"

It took a moment for everyone to realize what Jesse was talking about. Then, one-by-one, they started to laugh.

"I've got mine," announced Eli, pulling down his pants to reveal his Winnie the Pooh underpants.

This started everyone laughing again.

"Don't you understand?" Boaz pointed out to his younger brother. "People in those days wore their underpants all the time."

"Ugh!" Hannah complained. "Why do you tell him such dumb stuff?"

"Mom, she said the *dumb* word! Mom!"

"Okay, raise your hands if you want hamburgers!" Mrs. Zelkin said, deciding it was time to change the subject again. Four hands shot up!

Mrs. Zelkin sat the children down in the restaurant, and then — you never saw kids wolf down hamburgers so fast. You'd think they hadn't eaten all day. Even so, not everyone could finish their seconds. Mrs. Zelkin wrapped the leftovers up for Skip, the puppy.

On the way home, Hannah yelled, "Stop!"

"What now?"

"Look, Mom, that store is selling poles for the sukkah. We have to have a bigger sukkah this year."

"Yeah," Boaz agreed with Hannah — a first!

"Okay, let's do this quickly," Mrs. Zelkin said, although she knew from experience that things always took more time than she expected.

Hannah quickly calculated how many extra poles they would need: eight.

"Why eight?" asked Boaz, doubting Hannah's math abilities. "I counted six."

"No, dummy. Eight. See?" Hannah sketched a sukkah for Boaz. "You forgot two of the poles at the bottom, along the ground."

"No dummies, kids," Mrs. Zelkin warned. "And can we make some progress here?

"How much does each pole cost?" she asked the owner.

"Fifteen shekels," Hannah interjected, "That's one hundred and twenty shekels all together."

Mrs. Zelkin paid the storekeeper. Hannah and Boaz helped him tie the poles to the top of the car.

"Children, you've done an excellent job," their mother said. "I'm so proud of you. Now, let's get home!"

Later, at home, everyone was bubbling over to tell their father all that had happened.

The children all spoke at once. What Mr. Zelkin managed to understand was that Eli ran away, Jesse ran away, Eli showed his underwear and saw a giant Poly Pockets, Hannah went crazy for fabrics, Boaz saw a Magritte painting he liked, they all ate hamburgers, and a good time was had by all.

Skip was bubbling over, too. He had missed the children, and was licking Eli, jumping on Jesse, and tugging at Boaz's sleeve. He got the leftover hamburgers as a prize, which he wolfed down — faster than the kids had.

Mr. Zelkin went to unload the sukkah poles from

130

the roof of the car.

"Wait, Dad, it's okay. I'll do it," Hannah said.

"That's a big job, young lady. Are you sure you don't need help?"

"Not at all!" Hannah went out to the car, untied the poles, and began to unload them all by herself.

"Move over Hannah, I'm helping anyway," her father ordered, adding a hug.

But Hannah wouldn't let him. In fact she wouldn't even let anyone carry them into the shed. It was only after she promised to carry them one at a time that her father agreed to let her do it herself.

The shed was in the far corner of the garden. All the sukkah accessories and equipment were stored there.

"Don't you think you're overdoing it? Let someone help you," Mrs. Zelkin pleaded.

"No, thank you," Hannah replied emphatically. "Let me do this myself." She wiped the sweat from her brow and continued working.

For Mrs. Zelkin, the museum trip had been a much needed break from the cooking, planning, cleaning and shopping before the High Holidays. Every year they needed to buy new clothes, tablecloths, a set of drinking glasses (a set of eight became a set of two almost overnight), at least one siddur, a serving dish, and, sometimes, another silver cup. Every year the children helped polish silver, and get the house ready for the Holiday. And every year they had a house full of company.

Some years, their grandparents, aunts and uncles came to visit for the Holidays. Other years, friends came from around the world, or just from around the corner. Whoever came was always welcome, and everyone had fun. This year they were expecting friends from far and near: some for Rosh Hashanah, some for Sukkot, some would be sleeping over, and some would walk in for just one meal.

During the two days of Rosh Hashanah, Hannah spent a lot of time in the synagogue praying with the adults. At least, she tried to pray. On the second day of Rosh Hashanah, she found an old book on a shelf in the synagogue which, among other things, contained all the laws about building a sukkah. Sukkot was the holiday just after Yom Kippur that Hannah loved best.

Two days after Rosh Hashanah, Hannah asked her mother if she and a friend could go shopping at the mall.

"Shopping? With whose money?" her mother asked.

"Ours, of course."

"And who are you going with?"

"I'll meet Shani."

"All right, but be home before dark," Mrs. Zelkin told her.

That was one of the great advantages of living in Jerusalem. The children could be allowed to go out on their own, use public transportation, and shop by themselves, without adult supervision. Boaz and Hannah were always at the mall. Often, they would take the younger kids with them — at least Hannah would.

Hannah met her friend, Shani, downtown, and refused to tell her what she planned to buy.

"But you always tell me your secrets," Shani complained, trying to convince Hannah to tell her why they needed to go shopping.

"You'll see," Hannah smiled. She had saved up birthday and Hanukkah money for a few years, and had quite a bit to spend.

First, they went window shopping.

"Wait," Hannah said, when they passed a fabric store.

"What are you going to buy in here?" asked Shani. "You don't even know how to sew!"

Hannah came out five minutes later with a plastic bag. She showed her friend the fabric she had just bought.

"It's pretty fabric. What's it for?"

Hannah refused to tell Shani.

They continued walking, and came to a Persian style bazaar. Inside, the store was filled from floor to ceiling with carpets, fabrics, copper pots and kettles, and other things that looked like they belonged in a museum.

"What are you going to buy in there?" Shani asked. Her curiosity was getting the better of her. "Please tell me," she begged.

"Give me five minutes, and then I'll tell you," Hannah answered. When she came out from the bazaar, she was holding a paper bag.

"Let's get hamburgers and I'll tell you everything," Hannah suggested to Shani.

"Okay."

Over hamburgers, fries, and drinks, Hannah explained.

"We went to the Museum just before Rosh Hashanah. There was a wonderful exhibit on the Jews of Afghanistan, and there were wonderful fabrics on display. They had beautiful colors, and were decorated with ancient symbols. I got a great idea to redo our sukkah this year. Take a look." She opened the second bag.

"These fabrics are fabulous! Aren't they too fancy for a sukkah?" Shani asked.

"That's just the thing," Hannah explained. "I learned in school that the sukkah is a miniature Holy Temple. So, I thought I should try to use the kind of fabrics people used on walls in those times."

"*You* thought? Doesn't your mother know about this?"

"No, that's the other thing. This is all a surprise for the whole family."

"Wow, that's really something." Shani was surprised at Hannah's initiative, and by her take-over manner.

When Hannah returned home, she went straight to the shed in the garden. She hid the bags, neatly folded, on a stool behind the old sukkah fabric. Then she snuck out and went into the kitchen, without anyone knowing she'd been in the shed. She walked quietly past her father who was reading a magazine in the living room.

"How's the sukkah business?" he asked with a smile, closing the magazine. "I hear you've been busy buying a new wardrobe for Sukkot — with your own money, no less. I didn't know you were so wealthy."

Hannah smiled. Had her father seen her come in from the shed?

"I'm not wealthy," she explained. "I'm frugal."

"Kugel?" Jesse asked, entering the dining room. "Save me a piece," he commanded, running out.

Eli, who was obnoxiously trailing his big brother, came in and whispered something to his father.

"What did he say?" Hannah asked, once Eli had left.

"He said, he likes noodles," her father said, laughing, "but only in chicken soup." Hannah and her father both laughed. But Hannah was relieved more than amused. Clearly, her father had no idea what she was up to.

"People come and go, saying the strangest things," Mr. Zelkin said, paraphrasing from *Alice in Wonderland*.

"Living in this house is like playing telephone," Hannah observed.

The rest of that week, until right before Yom Kippur, Hannah would sneak out to the shed to look at her treasures. Once, Skip followed her out to the shed, and entered barking. He wagged his tail, and jumped on Hannah.

"There's nothing for you to eat here," she whispered to the dog. Skip wagged his tail even harder, knocking over one of Hannah's precious bags.

"Oh, you bad dog, you!" Hannah scolded. She folded up the fabric that had fallen out and placed the bag out of sight. Then, feeling sorry she had yelled at Skip, she petted him until he calmed down. She went to the door of the shed and, peeking out, found Boaz in front of her.

"What are you doing here?" he asked.

For a minute, she didn't know what to say. Then, it came to her.

"Skip chased a cat into the shed. I just brought him out," she said, pointing to Skip prancing out of the shed.

"Chasing a cat?" Boaz said, sarcastically. "The only thing he chases is his tail. He'd probably run the other way if he saw a cat nearby."

Then Boaz left.

"Close call," Hannah said to Skip, as she petted him. "Looks like you saved me, after all."

Late one night, Hannah had a dream about the sukkah. She dreamed that the sukkah was all finished. The poles had all been connected, and the fabric hung on the sides — they were the walls of the sukkah. The decorations were all up, hanging from the ceiling, and taped to the walls. The sukkah looked magnificent.

In the dream, Hannah was sitting in the sukkah when, suddenly, it began to transform into the Holy Temple. The walls became pure gold, and beautiful fabrics hung from the outside. There were steps leading up to an altar for sacrifices. There was a hush in the air. You could almost hear the silence.

The next morning, Hannah went out to the garden to try to visualize how the sukkah would look. She wanted it to be a miniature duplicate of the one she had dreamed of. To accomplish that, she knew there was a lot of hard work ahead of her.

That night, the fast of Yom Kippur, the holiest

day in the Jewish calendar, began. Hannah said she would try to fast for half a day. Boaz said he would try, too. As for the two little boys, they spent that night and the whole day of Yom Kippur eating, drinking and snacking. No matter how many times she told them she was fasting, they insisted on offering her food. They assured her it would make the day go "fast." Here she was, trying to take the day seriously, and her brothers were making her laugh.

Hannah spent most of the day in the synagogue. She did pray, but she also read the book with the laws about building a sukkah. She just couldn't resist it. Hannah wanted to build it correctly.

When Yom Kippur ended, Hannah and Boaz started helping their mother prepare the "break-the-fast" meal.

"Hey, that's where the word 'breakfast' comes from. 'Cause while you sleep, you don't eat. In the morning you break your fast." Boaz said, proud of himself.

"Keep stirring those eggs, Mr. Philoso-fool," Hannah told him.

"No sarcasm, now, children. It's a new year. Let's try to be pleasant," Mrs. Zelkin said.

From the other room, Jesse and Eli were singing "Avinu Malkeinu," one of the last songs of the Yom Kippur prayers. But it sounded like "Avinu Ameinu!" Hannah and Boaz began to laugh. The children were pronouncing the words very badly, changing the meaning of the whole song. Skip joined in, barking.

"He's the only one on key," Boaz observed.

"He's the only one who knows the words!" Hannah added.

"Could you keep it down, please? I have a headache from fasting," their mother yelled above the noise.

"I have an announcement," Hannah said, when things quieted down. "I'm going to be in charge of the sukkah this year. From A to Z, from Aleph to Tav, from one to a million!"

"Are you sure you can handle it?" her mother asked. "It's a big responsibility, and a lot of work."

"Sure I'm sure."

"I'll help," Boaz added.

"Okay, but I'm the boss."

"How come she gets to be the boss, Mom?" Boaz whined.

"'She' has a name," Hannah reminded him.

"How come the fabric lady gets to be boss?" Boaz teased.

"I'm staying out of this," their mother decided.

"Out of what?" Mr. Zelkin asked, as he walked in the door. "And Shana Tova to you all. May God grant us all a year of health and prosperity!"

"Hi, Dad," Hannah said. "I'm in charge of the

sukkah this year!"

"Hannah's always in charge. She always bosses me around," Boaz complained.

"I think I'll stay out of this, too!" Mr. Zelkin seconded.

"Shana Tova, dear," his wife said. "Have you noticed anything different about the way the children are fighting this year?"

"No," he answered.

"Neither have I," she agreed.

During dinner, Jesse and Eli continued to entertain everyone by singing holiday songs. Skip barked along. He got so excited, barking and wagging his tail, he forgot himself and leaped onto Mr. Zelkin's lap.

"Skip, behave yourself," Mr. Zelkin shouted, jumping up from his chair. Skip skipped onto the floor.

"He's just a dog, Dad," said Boaz.

"He's my friend," said Jesse. "Don't yell at him."

"He's my fwend, too," came Eli's echo. When he saw that his father was angry at Jesse for telling him what to do, Eli decided not to follow in his brother's dangerous footsteps. "You can yell at him all the time, Dad," he answered.

Mr. Zelkin took Skip outside, so they could finished dinner without further incident.

After dinner, Hannah said, "Every smart boss knows how to delegate responsibilities. Who wants to help build the sukkah?"

Just then the doorbell rang. It was Mr. Zelkin's friend, Aryeh.

"Someone say something about building a sukkah? I'm game!"

"Have you eaten yet?" asked Mrs. Zelkin.

"What, are you kidding? What's the difference? There's always room for more."

"Aryeh!" Mr. Zelkin exclaimed, happy to see his friend. "Glad you haven't lost your appetite, and after such a long fast, too!"

"Was his appetite lost," Jessie asked, worried.

"I got lost at the museum," Eli volunteered.

"Uncle Aryeh, where's your appetite?" Jessie wanted to know.

"Don't worry, kids," Aryeh assured them. "My appetite never strays far — or for too long. It's right here," he said, patting his stomach.

"Boaz, make Aryeh a sandwich, please," Mrs. Zelkin said. The rest of the family went out to the garden.

Boaz had piled baloney, salami and turkey onto a huge sandwich, with lettuce, mayonnaise and mustard. Aryeh took the sandwich and, with Boaz, followed the others outside.

"Aryeh, you eat. Everyone else, listen up," Hannah said, taking her role seriously.

"Are you sure we have to start tonight?" asked

Boaz. "We're all tired."

"Your brother has something there," Mr. Zelkin said.

"Please, Dad, we're at least supposed to start tonight. That's the law."

"Well, you can't argue with *The Law*!" Hannah's father proclaimed.

"Okay, everyone," continued Hannah. "We bought extra poles to double the size of last year's sukkah. As you know, a sukkah must be big enough to accommodate 18 people. That's *chai,* for life. A sukkah must have four sides, that's for the four winds, and because there are four children in our family. A sukkah should have 39 decorations. That's because there are 39 different things you need to do in the Holy Temple, and the sukkah is like the Temple."

Just then Mr. Zelkin interrupted, "I don't want to argue with *The Law*, but is this *The Law* according to the Talmud, or according to Hannah?"

Hannah couldn't understand why her father was making such a big deal about her creative license.

"Look, Dad, these are...uh... laws that I thought would help our family enjoy Sukkot more."

"All right, then, I'm sure we're all happy to do it your way, as long as everyone knows that there are God's Laws, and there are Hannah's laws."

"Hey, when do I get to make up my laws?" Boaz whined. "She gets to call me 'dummy' and gets to be in charge of the sukkah, AND gets to make up her own laws. That's not fair!"

"What law do you want to make, dear?" Mrs. Zelkin asked her son.

"I want to make a law that I don't have to go to school," Boaz quickly answered.

"Fine," his mother said.

Everyone turned to her. Boaz was all smiles, but it was clear that the other children wanted to present their own laws, as well.

"Hannah's laws are good for all of Sukkot," Mrs. Zelkin continued, "and your laws will be good for all of Sukkot."

"But I don't have school during Sukkot," Boaz protested.

"The defense rests," Mrs. Zelkin said, with a smile. Boaz began to pout.

"Okay. Now, where was I?" Hannah said, afraid to lose her audience. "Oh, yes. The sukkah is like the Temple, so I went out last week and spent some of my Hanukkah and birthday money on these new fabrics for the sides." Hannah pulled out the fabric she had bought with a flourish, spreading it out on the grass for everyone to see.

"Ooh!"

"Ahh!"

Everyone was suitably impressed.

"Wow!" said Aryeh, with his mouth full. "Those

are beautiful. But I think you should make clothes out of them for the holiday."

"Very funny," Hannah said, angrily, glaring at Aryeh.

"Just a thought," Aryeh said, meekly.

The fabrics looked a lot like the fabrics they had seen at the Jewish Museum. There were five-pointed stars, Stars of David, menorahs, sheaves of wheat and other designs on the fabric.

"Hannah, these are fabulous," said her father.

"You shouldn't have," said her mother.

"We'll pay you back," Mr. Zelkin added.

"That kid is really something," said Aryeh, smacking his lips as he finished the sandwich.

Together they all began to match up the poles. Some had slats at the ends. Others had small 'pockets' into which you put the slat of the connecting pole.

"Don't forget," Hannah announced, "we're still using some of the old fabric. You have to put the poles through the slits in the fabric at the top and bottom before you connect the poles. If you forget, we'll have to do it all over again. The new fabric we'll hang on top of the old, later."

"Yes sir!" Aryeh said, "I mean yes ma'am!"

"She's soooo bossy," Boaz said, rolling his eyes.

"Isn't it nice someone else is in charge of building the sukkah this year!" Mr. Zelkin said to his wife.

Slat into pocket, slat into pocket. Building the

sukkah took almost two hours.

While they were working, they heard distant hammering and banging. Neighbors up and down the street were beginning to build their sukkahs as well.

"Not bad," Hannah announced later, looking at the skeletal sukkah. "Thank you all for your time. I'll do the rest."

"You said I could help," Boaz reminded Hannah.

"Sure. Tomorrow."

"Hannah, you don't want my help hanging the new fabric, tomorrow?" her father asked.

"No thanks. Hey, be careful over there!" she yelled at Jesse and Eli. The boys and the dog were playing tag in the garden. Skip had banged into a sukkah pole, and the whole sukkah swayed.

"Why aren't you kids in bed yet?" Hannah yelled.

"Hannah, you may be in charge of the sukkah this year, but — guess who's still in charge of the kids?" her father reminded her. "This is their vacation, too, remember?"

Hannah looked a little downcast, but she knew her father was correct.

"As it happens to be," her father continued, with a smile, "it *is* their bedtime. All right, Eli and Jessie, into bed!" her father commanded.

That night, Hannah cut string into eight inch long

pieces to hang the decorations and fabric from. She sat on her bed, the ball of string in her lap and the pieces in a pile. Skip jumped up on the bed, grabbed the ball and headed out the bedroom door. He ran right into Mrs. Zelkin.

"Skip, stop it! Good night, Hannah. Bedtime was 15 minutes ago," she reminded Hannah, picking up the ball and handing it to her.

"Just five more minutes, okay, Mom?"

"Okay," her mother agreed. "I'm really proud of the job you're doing," she said, and gave her daughter a hug.

Hannah continued cutting pieces of string.

A few minutes later, "Hey, sweetheart, lights out," her father said, closing her light. "Good night."

The next day, Hannah got up bright and early to plan out her day. Then, she gathered her pieces of string, and went out to the garden. She carefully strung the new fabrics and hung them tightly between the poles. Hannah was examining her handiwork when her mother came outside.

"The sukkah looks beautiful," Mrs. Zelkin said.

"This is nothing, Mom. Wait until you see the decorations."

Hannah went inside, got scissors, construction paper, staples, glue and tape.

She began cutting the paper into strips.

"Hey, you said I could help," Boaz said.

"Well, then, help," Hannah told him. Together they cut strips, and began to connect them into a paper chain. Slowly, the chain grew longer and longer. It reached the floor, snaked up a chair, and down the other side. When it reached from one end of the room to the other, Hannah decided that they were done.

"It's long enough to drape just the way I want to," she said.

"Let's go out and hang it up now," Boaz suggested, as Jesse, Eli, and Skip ran in.

"Don't even think of running around in here now," Hannah warned, sounding a lot like her mother.

"But we want to help, too."

"Then follow me," Hannah said. It looked like a parade: Hannah, Boaz, Jesse, and Eli, all holding a huge paper chain snake, and Skip frolicking in the rear.

Once inside the sukkah, the two older children climbed on chairs and began to drape the chain around the wooden slats which made up the roof. The two younger children, and the dog, ran around underfoot.

"Hey, be careful over there," Hannah called to them. "This isn't a play room! This is a sukkah!"

"I'm king of the wild things!" Jesse yelled, running out of the sukkah. Eli ran after him, with the dog, tail wagging, skipping behind them.

While Hannah and Boaz were hanging and stretching the decorations, they could still hear the distant hammering of a neighboring sukkah. It was fun to feel like part of a larger picture. It seemed like everyone was building a sukkah.

When they finished hanging the paper chain, Hannah said, "Boaz, now it's time to get the *schach*." Schach is what makes up the roof of a sukkah. Hannah's family used slats, and put leafy branches or fronds on top of the slats.

"Do you know where we can get some branches? I didn't see any on my way home from school," Boaz stated.

"Well, if you had walked home the regular way, instead of stopping at your friend's house, you'd have seen what I saw. Down the block and around the corner are huge piles of branches just waiting to be dragged over here," Hannah said happily.

Every year, before Sukkot, the Jerusalem municipality prunes trees and cuts down branches, so that people can use them for their sukkah. But there is no home delivery. It's first come, first served.

The children walked out of the house.

"Can't I come too?" Jesse asked.

"Me, too," said Eli.

"No. You guys stay here. This is real hard work. The branches weigh more than you do. We'll have something for you to help us with when we get back,"

Hannah said.

"Aw, c'mon," Jesse whined.

"Hey, look, there's Skip. He has your stuffed dog!" Hannah said, pointing to the house. Jesse and Eli ran inside, ready to rescue Walter, their stuffed dog, from the jaws of Skip, their real dog. There was much barking and yelling, as Hannah and Boaz snuck away.

"We'd better hurry, or there won't be any schach left," Hannah said. She was nervous about finding enough branches to cover her sukkah.

"Yeah, I keep hearing hammering," Boaz pointed out. "I hope they're not looking for branches, too."

"Let's go faster," his sister said, beginning to run.

Around the block, there were piles of branches scattered on the sidewalk. Hannah and Boaz pulled, and tugged, and lugged, and somehow got all the branches they needed back to the front of their house, leaving a trail of twigs and leaves behind them. They even left some branches on the sidewalk for their neighbors.

As the children and their branches reached the house, there was a yell from behind them.

"Hey, kids, let me help ya!" It was Aryeh. He grabbed some of the branches and dragged.

When they finished piling the branches next to the sukkah, Boaz said, "I gotta take a break." He walked towards the house, breathing heavily.

"You always take breaks," Hannah called after him, teasingly.

"I bet you could use a break, too," Aryeh said. "I'm ready to rest, too." He went inside after Boaz.

Stubborn as ever, Hannah began trying to hoist the branches on top of the sukkah. She decided she didn't need help. She would do it all by herself. But the truth was that Hannah could barely lift even one branch by herself!

Hannah stood on a chair, and lifted up a branch. It was heavy work, and she was making very slow progress, when her father came home.

"Hi," he said. "Let me change, and I'll lend you a hand."

"Aryeh's here," Hannah told him.

"And I'll bet he's eating! I'll be right there to help you."

Hannah was grateful. Together, she and her father got the branches on top of the sukkah without mishap. Boaz had been watching, and finally decided to join them.

"We can use all the help we can get," his father told him. "Why did you let your sister do it by herself?"

"She insulted me," Boaz answered.

"I didn't insult you," Hannah said. "I characterized you," she explained.

"You see, Dad," Boaz exclaimed, doubly hurt.

"Not only did she insult me, she characterized me, too!"

"Hey, hold on there," their father said, looking at both of them. "Let's just build the sukkah, okay? It's a new year and already you're at each other's throats."

It was Mr. Zelkin's turn to change the subject, and he began singing a holiday song, as the three of them joined together in finishing the work. Aryeh came out to help, just as they were putting on the finishing touches.

The branches were carefully arranged on top of the sukkah, so that you could still see the stars through the schach.

"Hannah, it's incredible! You've all done a wonderful job!" Mrs. Zelkin said, when she saw the sukkah.

"It's still not finished, Mom," beamed Hannah.

"Well, don't overdo things. Don't you think there are enough decorations already?" The sukkah was starting to look like a colored paper forest.

"Aw, c'mon, Mom. I want to do it my way," Hannah replied.

Later that night, Hannah's father found her in the shed.

"What's going on here, young lady?"

"I'm doing inventory," Hannah explained. "There are 29 decorations already made, so I have ten more to make."

"You know, God wants us to enjoy building a sukkah. This seems like too much work for one person. And, anyway, you made up your own sukkah rules, so you can change them."

"I'm fine, Dad. Really."

"Aren't you tired? I'm bushed from putting up the branches."

"Well...."

"Well, now's a good time to stop."

The next day, Hannah was as busy as a beaver. She planned, and designed her decorations with great care. Her friend, Shani, had given her a few great ideas while they were in school. Hannah rushed through her homework, and began work on those last 10 decorations. She had learned to make sunbursts and lanterns in school. She had also designed three dimensional fruits. All these things were made of construction paper, cardboard, corrugated plastic, and tinsel. And all these things were strewn all over Hannah's bed — her workshop.

Hannah could hear Skip barking just outside her door. She was concentrating very hard, tracing, cutting, folding, and stapling. As she looked up from her work, Skip ran in, grabbed a lantern between his teeth, and ran out. The puppy wrestled with the paper lantern, and managed to get it stuck on his head. Frightened, he began to run around her room, barking.

"Look!" shouted Jesse, running in to find out what was happening. "Skip's king of the wild things!"

"A wild thing!" Eli screamed, joining the group. "Look out!"

"You're ruining everything," Hannah shouted, chasing after all three.

She caught Skip, and pulled the lantern off his head, tearing it as she did so. "You better stay out of my room. Jesse, play with Eli and Skip somewhere else, okay?" Hannah went back to her work.

Hannah was still hanging up the last of the decorations at 8:30 p.m. She had made the seven species of native fruits and grains of Israel: wheat, barley, grapes, dates, olives, pomegranates, and figs. Also displayed were the four species associated with Sukkot: palm, myrtle, willow, and the citron — Etrog — a fragrant citrus fruit. Pictures of the seven traditional 'Ushpizin,' visitors from the Bible — Abraham, Isaac, Jacob, Joseph, Moses, Aaron, and David — hung together on the fabric walls. Paper chains, and other creative and decorative paper foldouts, were hung, strung, draped, and taped all around. She had created most of them herself, and was very proud.

"This is just beautiful," her father said. "But you have plenty of time. Sukkot doesn't start for another two days."

"Dad, I'll be finished in a minute. I still have so many other things to do."

When Hannah finished, she sat down in the middle of the sukkah, just like in her dream. She was expecting the walls to turn into gold, and steps to an altar to appear. Of course, none of that happened. Yet, she still felt as though she had helped build the Temple, somehow.

From the kitchen door, her mother and father watched her quietly sitting. They understood Hannah's special need to be in charge of the sukkah, and were very proud of her accomplishment.

The next day, everyone "oohed" and "aahed" at Hannah's wonderful sukkah. Shani came over to see what Hannah had been up to all week.

"Wow! This is really great! It's even better than our sukkah," she admitted.

One after another, friends and neighbors came to see Hannah's wonderful sukkah. One neighbor must have told another, because they kept coming in, admiring, and complimenting Hannah. Aryeh came by too. He was full of praise.

"I can't believe you did this all by yourself!" he exclaimed.

"Well, mostly," Hannah said.

"You can come decorate my house after the Holiday!" Aryeh winked at Hannah.

Boaz came running in, "I've just been to two other sukkahs on this block. Theirs don't even compare to ours!"

"You mean mine," Hannah corrected him.

"It's ours," Boaz said emphatically. An argument was about to begin.

"I hate to interrupt," Mr. Zelkin intervened, "but it is *our* sukkah, Hannah. It's for the whole family. You know, when you were younger, I made the sukkah all by myself."

"Of course, it was nowhere as beautiful as this," Mrs. Zelkin was quick to add.

"We all sat in it," her father continued, "and I never thought of it as mine."

Humbled, Hannah walked out of the sukkah. Her father could see that she was sulking.

"As a matter of fact, this is the first year I *haven't* built the sukkah in, I don't know how long!" he called out after her. "Thanks for giving me a break!" he added. Hannah smiled, but didn't let her father see.

The sukkah was for living in. So, now they had to bring in the table and chairs. Aryeh helped the

Zelkins move the dining room table into the sukkah. Boaz brought in the chairs, carrying them, one at a time, over his head, pretending he was a weight-lifter. By accident, he knocked into one of the poles holding up the sukkah. The whole thing swayed.

"Please be careful," his father whispered. "If your sister thinks anything's been moved even a fraction, she'll get upset."

"I want to help, too," Jesse said, grabbing his chair from his room and dragging it across the floor.

"Me, too," said Eli. He found a lounge chair and began to tug at it.

"Let's be careful, or —" Mr. Zelkin warned the kids.

"I heard that," Hannah interrupted, rushing into the sukkah. "What's going on in here?"

Jesse and Eli both ran into the sukkah, dragging their chairs. Skip chased after them. The sukkah swayed as they banged into one pole after another.

"Oh, no!" Hannah yelled. "Get that dog out of here! Stop banging into the poles!"

But it was too late.

Some of the slats began raining down into the sukkah, as the sukkah itself began to sway to one side. Skip kept jumping up, trying to catch the slats in his mouth. The paper chain began to rip in dozens of places. Boaz was trying to tie the ripped ends together, but the slats kept banging him on his head.

Aryeh saw that the sukkah was about to fall over, and he braced himself against the far end, pushing and forcing the sukkah to straighten itself.

Unfortunately, Aryeh was stronger than he thought. Rather that straighten the sukkah, he pushed it so hard, it began to lean the *other* way. A fresh barrage of slats and branches bombarded those inside. This time, however, Aryeh had no time to shift to the other side of the sukkah. His own weight and momentum forced him forward onto the wall of the sukkah, which slowly — but inexorably — leaned closer and closer to the floor. As he was bent half-way forwards, Aryeh suddenly let out a loud, "Oh no!" and fell, with a crash, onto the wall, leveling it.

Jessie and Eli had seen the fall coming and had run outside the sukkah. There, they found two chairs and sat down, looking like an audience watching a play. They clapped and shouted, "Yea!" when the sukkah finally collapsed.

When the smoke cleared, everyone was standing except Aryeh. Skip had managed to catch a slat and was jumping and barking amid the ruins of the sukkah.

All this occurred in the space of two to three minutes.

"Oh, no! My sukkah is ruined!" Hannah cried. She had run into the sukkah behind everyone else, and almost crashed into Aryeh.

"It's our sukkah, Hannah, remember?" Boaz called to her, holding what was left of two pieces of the paper chain.

"Actually, it looks pretty funny," Mr. Zelkin noted. "Aryeh, hold that pose while I take your picture!"

Hannah didn't find anything amusing. She ran back into the house, crying.

Mr. Zelkin, Aryeh, and Boaz looked over the damage, and silently set to work. One sukkah pole was bent out of shape, so they made the sukkah a bit smaller, and used the outside wall of the house for the fourth wall of the sukkah.

"You don't need all four walls to have a kosher sukkah," Boaz assured them.

"Well, I'm glad you know so much about the laws of a sukkah," his father complimented. "Did they also teach you some songs for Sukkot?"

They sang Holiday songs together as they re-hung the new fabrics, and salvaged what they could of the paper chains. Aryeh and Boaz set the table upright and, all together, they carefully brought in the rest of the chairs. They didn't even get close to a pole.

When they were finished, there were less than Hannah's original 39 decorations in the sukkah. There were fewer species on the walls, and a shorter paper chain. The sukkah could hold 12 people at most, not 18 as planned.

"Come on, Hannah, you'll see. It really looks lovely," Mrs. Zelkin said, coaxing Hannah out of her room.

"But it won't be the same," Hannah complained.

"So what? No two sukkahs are the same, but that doesn't mean they all aren't beautiful. Actually, this new version, in some ways, is even prettier than the first." Mrs. Zelkin was trying to use logic on Hannah. It seemed to be working. Hannah was curious as to how this battle-scarred sukkah could possibly be nicer than the first one. Hannah went to inspect the sukkah with her mother.

Yes, they'd made the sukkah a bit smaller, Hannah saw. And to her disappointment, some of the decorations were gone, even some of the important ones. The sukkah no longer complied with Hannah's set of laws. But it was still a lovely, large, and well-decorated sukkah. It still bore Hannah's handiwork.

There was one thing, however, which *was* better than the first sukkah.

Over the door to the sukkah, her family had put up a sign in bright red, so that everyone could see:

> # A Hannah and Company Production

"Well? What do you think, now?"

"I guess it's okay," Hannah said, holding back a smile.

"You only guess?" Aryeh said. "It's wonderful. Admit it!"

"Yes, it's a beautiful sukkah," Hannah had to admit, with a growing smile. Her parents gave her a big hug.

Up to one hour before Sukkot began, neighbors were still coming in to admire Hannah's sukkah. Hannah found herself telling them the story of how hard she had worked and planned, and how in just a few short minutes, the whole sukkah had turned topsy-turvy. And, how her father and everyone had fixed everything up. By the end of the story, Hannah found herself laughing with her neighbors at the thought of the ceiling caving, Aryeh on the floor, and Jessie and Eli applauding.

Hannah called her friend Shani on the telephone to tell her the story, too. Then, when everyone was gone, she went out to the sukkah, and sat quietly for just a few minutes. Yes, that feeling of quiet was still there. Her sukkah would still remind them all of the Holy Temple.

At dinner the first night of Sukkot, there were twelve people sitting in the sukkah. There was plenty of room. Everyone admired the new fabrics and the decorations. During dinner, Mr. Zelkin gave a small talk about Sukkot and its significance. He also told the whole story of Hannah's sukkah all over again, for those who hadn't heard it before.

At the end of the story, when everyone had finished laughing, Mr. Zelkin said, "We all have a lesson to learn here. The lesson is that, when we have the right intentions, things will come out all right in the end. The important thing is to do the best job you can, and enjoy yourself while doing it. This is the holiday of joy, and that is how we should celebrate it — joyously!

"I'm sure there's more to learn from Hannah's experience, too, like about letting dogs run into the sukkah, and about letting little boys carry chairs much too big for them, and," Mr. Zelkin glanced at Aryeh, "about leaning left when you should be leaning right. But I'd rather not talk about it!" Everybody laughed again.

When the meal was almost done, Hannah asked to say a few words, as well. With an air of authority she welcomed the guests to the sukkah, emphasizing that it was a family effort. Then she said, "Now, close your eyes and just imagine that the sukkah is the Temple, enjoying the beauty that filled the Temple. That's the feeling I wanted everyone to get when we hung up these special fabrics."

The sukkah was silent, and, this time too, just like those other times, Hannah could feel the hush all around her. After a moment, she asked everyone to open their eyes.

All through the week of Sukkot, the Holiday guests admired the sukkah. Hannah was careful to remember to remind everyone that it was the family's sukkah, but, yes, she did most of the work, and was willing to take the lion's share of the credit.

Aryeh came for dinner a few times, claiming he just had to admire the sukkah again and again. Shani brought over a few more friends to show off Hannah's sukkah. Hannah reminded them, too, that it was the family's sukkah. But Shani liked to show off her friend's work anyway, and gave Hannah full credit for everything.

On the last night of the Holiday, there was a terrible thunderstorm. This was the first rain of the new year. It was said to be a blessing, because on Sukkot you pray for the harvest rains to begin, and for the dry season to end.

The rain came down in torrents. You can imagine what the rain did to the sukkah. The decorations became soaked with water. Some hung down limply, others tore off altogether. Colors from the construction paper lanterns ran everywhere. The schach finally began to blow off the top of the sukkah.

But since they wouldn't need the sukkah until next year, Hannah quietly watched the weather beating down on the slowly disintegrating sukkah. This time, she did not shed tears. But she was still sad to see her sukkah disappear.

Aryeh was with the family that night, enjoying Mrs. Zelkin's good cooking, and watching the rain with Hannah. He put his hand on her shoulder.

"Hey, Hannah, stop worrying. You know what they say:

That's the way the sukkah crumbles!"

Nothing to SNEEZE *At*

William P. "Bill" Lazarus is a resident *of Daytona Beach, Florida, where he lives with his wife, Kathleen, and daughter, Maia. He teaches Sunday School at his Temple, and has taught religious history at Stetson University and Daytona Beach Community College.*

Bill has a Master's degree in journalism from Kent State University and spent 12 years as a newspaper reporter. He is now Director of Public Information/Cultural Affairs for the City of Daytona Beach Shores and editor of Halifax Magazine.

Maia, Bill's daughter, recently became Bat Mitzvah. She has a variety of allergies, which inspired this story.

*D*anny Wisener carefully judged the steps leading to the *bima,* the raised platform in front of the Ark, where his parents and the Rabbi stood. He was sure that no one, not even the high schoolers, had ever stood in front of these three steps and leaped straight to the top. No one had probably even thought of it before. He could hop over the first one from a standing start, with no trouble. The second one seemed a bit of a stretch, but possible. Hopping over the third one in a single magnificent leap? That was the challenge! He readied himself.

Danny Wisener, a 13-year-old boy getting ready for his Bar Mitzvah, was going to make history.

Rocking slowly back and forth, Danny could hear his heart pounding in his ears. Sweat appeared across his forehead. His muscles tensed. He stared at the steps, willing himself to leap through the air and land gracefully on the top. He could almost see himself flying. People would be amazed, he told himself. He would bring his friends here and duplicate the great feat. No one would be able to match his jump. He knew it.

He was ready.

Taking a deep breath, Danny jumped.

He easily cleared the first step. He flew past the second step. Then, as he was soaring, his right foot caught the lip of the third step. He landed with a thud, lost his balance, and tumbled backwards down the stairs. He almost rolled onto his sister's lap. Rachel was sitting in the first row of the Synagogue, and laughing at him.

"Danny!" his mother cried.

"Sorry," Danny apologized.

He really wasn't. He was disappointed. He had almost jumped all three steps. How far had he gone? He tried to estimate. That had to be 6 feet. No, 8 feet. Maybe it was 10 feet. It really must have been a world record, even if he only jumped over two-and-a-half steps.

He would just have to try again. He glanced up. His parents were listening to the Rabbi, who was explaining something. Danny didn't care, even if the instructions were for his own Bar Mitzvah. He had seen enough Bar Mitzvahs. He knew what to do.

It was more important to jump these steps. That was his task this Sunday afternoon. His Bar Mitzvah was almost a week away. He had memorized his Haftorah, and he had learned the prayers. Or, at least, he knew them as well as he could ever learn them. What he didn't know was if he could set a world record in the category of *Bima-Stair Jumping*.

He picked himself off the carpet, and walked to the stairs. They seemed so high. He took another deep breath. At least he was dressed in gym shoes and jeans. He wouldn't ever be able to make the winning leap in a suit. And when else would he have a chance? He was usually dressed up when he went to Synagogue. The few times he came here in casual clothes, people were in the sanctuary, or there were lots of children for a school assembly. Right now, no one else was here, watching, except Rachel. No, Danny decided, it had to be now, or never.

He nervously counted the steps again, and dried his hands on his pants. Jumpers were given at least two chances to set a world record, weren't they? Danny wasn't sure, but one more chance seemed fair. And these steps were so high.

He readied himself again.

"My brother, the bully frog," Rachel whispered behind him.

"Quiet!" Danny hissed at her. "Don't you see there's a rehearsal going on?"

"I'm not the one jumping up stairs," she replied.

"That's because you can't," Danny told her.

"That's because I'm not a frog," she teased.

He ignored her comment. A world record holder didn't have to listen to his little sister, especially if dressing a Barbie doll was her idea of *extreme* excitement.

Danny took another breath, expanding his chest as much as he could. The air would propel him upward. He waited a second to clear his thoughts. He pressed his shoes hard against the carpet, bent his knees, and threw himself forward.

Up, up, and away!

This time, he easily cleared the first two steps. His feet reached the top step. He felt the hard wood beneath his shoes. He tried to catch his balance, but couldn't. Instead, he was thrown forward, toward the three elegant chairs alongside the Ark. He banged into the closest one. He tried to use his hands to stop himself, but only managed to bounce backwards into the Rabbi's podium.

The podium teetered under his weight, then toppled forward, pulling the microphone cord with it. Books that had been sitting on top of the podium, flew in various directions. Papers scattered like large snowflakes. Danny came to rest against the base of the podium, which was balanced above the ground at an odd angle, held in place by the thin cord that stretched from the microphone into a hole in the floor.

"Danny!" Mr. Wisener yelled. He rescued the podium and repositioned it in its proper place. He signaled urgently at Rachel who, with a great show of exhaustion, collected the fallen books and papers.

Danny straightened himself and waited, triumphantly, by the podium. He was waiting to be congratulated on his record-breaking *Bima-Stair Jumping* success. He smiled proudly, just the way all those Olympic athletes did when they won a medal.

"Oh, Danny," his mother sighed. "Can't you sit still for a minute? Are you going to be this restless at the Bar Mitzvah?"

"I jumped three steps," Danny announced, with a flourish.

"He's a frog," Rachel insisted. "A big, ugly bully frog."

"We really do have to get serious," Rabbi Gordon advised. "Good thing I wasn't taking out the Torah."

Danny stood up. Obviously, they did not appreciate his record. Maybe he should repeat his feat for them. Then he felt a twinge of pain where his shoulder had collided with the wooden podium. He decided to be satisfied with his success. If he jumped once, he could jump again another day. Maybe there was something else he could do? Hurdle the rows of wooden benches? That looked interesting. He could already see himself running toward the first row, grabbing the first chair, and flinging himself over.

This rehearsal was going to be a lot of fun.

"Please come here," the Rabbi called, interrupting Danny's thoughts.

Danny frowned. The Rabbi wanted him to stand on the bima across from his parents. How boring, Danny thought, especially when there were so many wonderful things he could do. Could he shimmy up the rough wall next to the Ark? There was a real challenge! He could picture himself halfway to the ceiling. He felt a familiar itching in his hands. They were ready to grab onto that rocky surface, and start climbing.

"Over here, Danny," Mrs. Wisener ordered. She took his hand, and led him to the designated spot. She was always dressed so formally, Danny thought to himself. She couldn't jump up any stairs. She probably never had. And his father — Danny glanced at him — he wasn't an athlete, just a writer. Writing didn't require any jumping, although his father said he did jump through hoops for his boss. Danny had jumped through a hoop once. It was boringly easy.

They just didn't understand.

He tapped his feet impatiently. The Rabbi approached the large doors of the Ark. He was saying something about how the doors were once part of a barn, but had been removed and brought to the Temple. Danny was not impressed. He couldn't wait to go home and tell his friends about jumping up all those steps, and climbing halfway to the ceiling, and hurdling those seats; the last two were still on his Olympic Trials list.

Behind him, Rachel was making funny faces, and squeaky noises, trying to make him laugh. He ignored her. But he wouldn't forget. Just wait until she had her Bat Mitzvah. Besides, she couldn't appreciate his talent. She was so dumb.

"Danny," the Rabbi said. "I'm going to take out a Torah and give it to your father. He'll pass it to your mother, who will give it to you." He looked hard at Danny. "This is very important. You have to pay attention."

Danny sighed. This rehearsal was taking a very bad turn. He felt a sneeze starting, stifled it, and tried to appear interested.

He wasn't. Instead, he began to imagine what was going on inside the closed Ark. He could picture the Ark opening, and then — nothing! Wouldn't it be funny if the Torah had disappeared, as if by magic? Then he, Danny Wisener, magician extraordinaire, would wave his hand, and the Torah would reappear.

He would put on a great show. The Rabbi would stand in front of the Ark; his parents would open those large doors. Then, when the empty Ark was revealed, the Rabbi, finally at a loss for words, would say, "Oops!"

Danny could imagine how the congregation would react. Women would faint. Men would shout. There would be pandemonium. People would peer into the Ark, scratch their heads, scream, and cry. Then he'd calmly walk to the front of the bima. He would bow to the congregation, holding a large black hat in his hand, and wearing a cape, with a big Jewish star on it. He'd have to be careful not to tip the hat or all the rabbits would hop out.

Then, he would wave his wand, and say the

173

magic words, and...Danny stopped. Magic words? He shivered. Would they have to be in Hebrew? That would be awful. He didn't know enough Hebrew. "You'll regret not studying as much as you should," his mother had often told him. She was right. What's a Jewish magician without Hebrew words? A fake, that's what he is.

In desperation, Danny blinked the image away. The Rabbi reached for the great doors of the Ark. Danny prayed the Torah would be inside.

The Rabbi pulled on the great doors. They extended at least 12 feet high, yet moved easily on special hinges. He was talking a lot, perhaps trying to keep everyone relaxed. Danny could barely hear him. A silence had filled his ears. He could only see the Ark doors slowly begin to open.

The Torahs appeared, three of them in a row, resting against the back wall. They were all dressed up in their fancy silver ornaments, waiting to be touched. Danny couldn't wait to run his hands over them.

Until now, he had been too young to actually carry the Torah. The only thing he was allowed to do was run up and kiss the Torah, as a grownup carried it through the Synagogue on Shabbat. Danny envied him. Imagine being able to hold that beautiful scroll, and those incredible, shiny ornaments.

Danny tried to concentrate. The Rabbi started

to pass the Torah to Mr. Wisener. But once again, Danny's imagination took hold. He closed his eyes and daydreamed about the Torah being handed to him. It seemed light, but suddenly it squirmed and fell through his arms. It didn't touch the ground, but landed on its wooden handles, which had turned into legs. The scroll sprinted down the steps, across the carpet, and down the aisle. Danny chased it, as the ornaments flew off. The Torah screeched around the Synagogue like a crazed race car. Danny tried to catch up, but it kept racing ahead, those little legs making great time.

Danny saw Rachel laughing at him as he tried to catch the speeding scroll. His mother fainted. Danny watched her fall to the bima and lay there. His father was racing around, too, but he was shouting, "Water! Water!" to spill on her. Everyone was shouting. The police were rushing into the Synagogue. The Torah was still circling the back of the sanctuary. Danny knew he had to stop it. His mother had wanted everything to be perfect. He tried to catch the Torah, but it was too fast.

"Danny?" his mother whispered under her breath. He blinked, awake again. She was holding out the Torah.

He swallowed. His hands reached for the Torah and pulled it towards him. He felt the soft outer cover against his cheek, the firm wooden handles pressing against his body, heard the jangle of the ornamental crowns as they banged lightly against each other, and then felt the weight of the Torah against his shoulder.

Danny hugged it lovingly.

And sneezed.

The sneeze just erupted from him. His eyes watered. He sneezed again, and again, and again. Each sneeze shook his body. These were not simple sneezes, the polite sneezes someone might stifle by scrunching his nose. No, these were massive sneezes, bigger than the Ark's doors, bigger than anything known to Man. He felt the Torah jump in his arms as the sneezes erupted. His head snapped backward, his hair rushing forward to cover his eyes. His sister had to hold onto the side of her chair to avoid being flung against a wall.

"Wow," he heard Rachel exclaim.

"Amen," the Rabbi mumbled under his breath.

Danny turned his head away from the Torah. It wasn't heavy, but his hands were trembling. He sneezed at least three or four more times. His body suddenly felt weak.

"God bless you," the Rabbi said, a note of awe in his voice.

Abruptly, the Torah was gone. Danny felt the loss of the scroll deeply. In the distance, he could hear the enticing ring of the bells, as the Rabbi hurried to return the scroll to the Ark. Then, his ears became completely clogged. His mother was wiping his nose with a hanky. He turned away from her and sneezed again. His head ached. He wanted to sit down. His legs barely responded as he struggled towards the first row of seats. Finally, gratefully, he plopped down near Rachel.

His mother sat next to him. He could feel her anxious gaze, but his own eyes were filled with tears. He sneezed again.

"You won't do that during the service, will you?" Mrs. Wisener asked, pleading.

Danny tried to shake his head. Instead, he sneezed again.

"Nerves," Mr. Wisener decided. "I knew a man who sneezed whenever he was nervous. He was a knife-thrower. Lost his partner during the big sneeze of '94." His father laughed, and Danny joined him.

"Are you nervous?" Mrs. Wisener asked, seriously.

Danny shook his head. He didn't think he was nervous. Abruptly, he felt whatever had caused his attack was gone. He took a deep breath and smiled.

"I'm all right," he announced.

"Maybe you're getting the flu," his mother said, touching Danny's forehead.

Danny shrugged her off. That was embarrassing. He stood up. His legs were strong again. "I don't know what happened," he said.

"You sneezed," Rachel reported. "A lot."

"Rachel," Mrs. Wisener said, sharply.

"Do you want to try again?" the Rabbi asked Danny.

"I think he's got the sneezing down pat," his sister quipped.

Danny nodded eagerly, and bounded onto the bima. Whatever had caused the problem had disappeared. His head was clear. His nose had dried. He felt very good. The problem couldn't have been his nerves. He had just been very excited. He smiled confidently at his father, who didn't seem to share Danny's confidence.

"I'm ready," Danny said.

The Rabbi smiled, too. "I'll take the Torah from the Ark and give it to your father. He'll hand it to your mother," he explained again.

The Torah was passed along. His mother took it gingerly. She sniffed it, and shrugged slightly. Then, careful so as not to muss her dress, she gave it to Danny.

Once again, he took it eagerly. He waited to see if he would sneeze. Nothing. Not even a tickle. He pulled the Torah close to his body.

"Ah-ah-ah-CHOO!" Danny sneezed.

This sneeze was even more powerful than the ones before. The eternal light flickered. The large bronze memorial plaques, held by thick screws on the wall, vibrated.

"Tornado!" Rachel yelled. "Everyone to the shelters!"

"Ah-ah-ah-CHOO," Danny sneezed again. The front door to the sanctuary flipped opened. People in the hallway outside stopped in their tracks. Mothers grabbed their children and held them close. Young kids started to cry. One old man was searching frantically for his toupe'. The massive doors of the Ark trembled. The Rabbi lunged to rescue the Torah.

"My son, the bazooka," Mr. Wisener said, barely able to keep from laughing. "Let us know before you reload."

"Danny," Mrs. Wisener wailed. "How could you?"

"I'm sure the boy didn't mean it," the Rabbi said soothingly. "You know, sneezing is a sign of life. Elisha the prophet once saved a young boy who was dead. The boy came back to life by sneezing seven times."

Rachel added, "Seven of Danny's sneezes and that prophet would have been *blown* to kingdom come!"

"Stop it!" Mrs. Wisener said. "I don't care if he meant it or not. He can't sneeze during the service. What will people think? And at the party. If he starts sneezing, he'll blow down all the decorations."

"Now, Marilu," Mr. Wisener said.

"Can we give him a pill?" Mrs. Wisener asked.

"Just shoot him," Rachel suggested, "or put cotton up his nose. That way, he'll blow his brains out."

"He doesn't even have a handkerchief," Mrs. Wisener cried, ignoring her daughter.

Danny felt the cloud that filled his brain begin to drain away. Just as quickly as the sneezing fit started, it ended.

"I think he's allergic to the Torah," suggested Mr. Wisener.

"It smelled musty to me," Mrs. Wisener added. "He doesn't do well with mold."

"Allergic to the Torah?" the Rabbi wondered aloud. He was still holding the scroll. He sniffed it, and wrinkled his nose.

"Can he use something else?" Mrs. Wisener asked. "Does he have to hold it? Is there any other Torah in there?" She was wringing her hands.

"I've never had anything like this happen before," Rabbi Gordon said.

"You've never had the Sneeze King have a Bar Mitzvah here before," Rachel said. She looked very happy.

Danny was not happy. The miracle jump of just a few minutes ago was now a memory. He felt really upset. Tears gathered in his eyes. This was worse than burping unexpectedly in class. This was worse than anything in recent memory. His shoulders slumped. He stumbled to a seat, and sat down. He bent over, and stared at the floor.

Mrs. Wisener sat next to him. "Danny," she said, "maybe we can do something else. We'll just skip this part. No one will know."

"I'm sorry, Mrs. Wisener," Rabbi Gordon said. "Danny has to read the Torah."

"Danny is different," Mrs. Wisener said, defiantly. "If it makes him sneeze, he just won't do it."

"Marilu," Mr. Wisener said. He glanced at the Rabbi, and then at his wife.

"Arthur," Mrs. Wisener said. "If it makes him sick, we're not going to make him do it."

"Mrs. Wisener," the Rabbi said quietly. "Danny has studied very hard. I am sure he wants to read from the Torah."

Danny rubbed his eyes. If he could skip his Torah reading, maybe sneezing wasn't so bad. He tweaked his nose, trying to evoke one more sneeze.

"Give him binoculars," Rachel suggested. "He can read at a distance."

Mrs. Wisener actually seemed to consider that idea for a moment. She shook her head. "None of the other children did that. I think we should just skip this part. Leave the Torah in the Ark, and let's just do the rest of the ritual."

"No," Rabbi Gordon said. "Please remember what a Bar Mitzvah is all about."

"We know what it's all about," Mrs. Wisener said.

"It's about showing off your children. It marks the last time your child has to go to Hebrew School.

"Marilu," Mr. Wisener said, trying to stop her.

"Oh, let's be serious," Mrs. Wisener continued. "Do you really think the kids care about this? They want presents. They want a big party. It's a competition. For the kids, and for the parents. Now, we've invested thousands of dollars in Danny's Bar Mitzvah. I bought two new dresses. Rachel has a new dress. Arthur has a new suit. We've rented the Tangiers ballroom. We've invited 250 people. We are not going to let a sneeze stop that."

Rabbi Gordon held up a hand. "We'll try again, Tuesday," he said, softly. He put the Torah back into the Ark, and closed the big doors. They slid noisily. "I really don't want to argue about it now," he said. Then he stepped down from the bima and walked to the back of the sanctuary.

The Wiseners watched him go. The Rabbi looked like an old man as he left the sanctuary.

"Notice he didn't contradict me," Mrs. Wisener pointed out. She touched Danny's shoulder. "No more sneezing. It's mind over matter."

"Yes, Mom," Danny said. He glanced back at the Ark as everyone started to leave. He never wanted to see what was inside the Ark again. He never even wanted to be in a Synagogue again, even if it was for *The World Cup Bima-Stair Jump*!

Danny tried to sneeze again. He sucked in a big breath, and held it, hoping it would stimulate his sneeze center. Nothing happened. He breathed through his nose. Same results. He sighed. He had spent the rest of Sunday, and all day at school Monday, trying to recreate the sneezes that blew away the rehearsal. He simply couldn't do them.

Yet, he kept thinking about them. Would he sneeze again this evening when he met with Cantor Roseland for singing practice? The thought was intriguing. The Cantor would start singing, and he'd create a gale that would smash his notes against the back wall. The Cantor would stare at him with his hands on his hips, the way he did when Danny forgot to bring his music or tried to slip in an extra high note during rehearsal. That would be funny. He was so nasty, always complaining about the way Danny pronounced words. It was Hebrew, after all. What did he expect?

If he could just feel a sneeze coming on and aim correctly, maybe he could blow the Cantor into Lake Michigan.

He could envision the Cantor suddenly caught

up in the wind blast, arms flailing, glasses flying, his hair standing on end as he sailed away.

Then, he thought of another sneeze blowing the Rabbi's *kippah* into the congregation, sending old Mr. Drabney's thick glasses landing onto Mrs. Kraut's permanently tweaked nose.

His pleasure was tempered by the thought of what would happen if he sneezed during his Bar Mitzvah ceremony. He had seen the anxious look on his mother's face. She'd be watching him to see that moment when a sneeze suddenly seemed imminent. She'd rush onto the bima and thrust a hanky at him. Danny almost cringed at that thought. He'd be so embarrassed. Of course, she'd be too late. His nose would have lift off, and the sneeze would rocket into the sanctuary.

But what about the party, afterwards. No one would get near him at the party. They'd all be afraid of being sent flying with a misdirected sneeze.

Actually, he smiled, the whole idea was pretty appealing. He could be a kind of carnival ride. Kids could step up and be sneezed into flight. Of course, he would have to be able to sneeze on cue.

But, how was he supposed to do that?

Nothing seemed to work, not even some frilly, ticklish-looking thing he borrowed from his sister's Barbie doll. Besides, he wasn't sure he wanted people at his Bar Mitzvah to be sneezed into orbit. Maybe they'd take their presents with them.

Danny sighed. He'd better figure out a way to stop sneezing. If he was allergic to the Torah, he'd have to wear an anti-sneeze device, like a mask. That made him sit up. He could look like Batman. That would justify jumping up those steps, too. Or maybe he could wear a Spiderman costume. He could swing along the rafters and drop down on a rope.

The image was thrilling, better even than sneezing. Danny began to get that old feeling of excitement. But, it faded quickly. His parents wouldn't appreciate all the effort he was going to.

Was there an anti-sneezing pill? He had never heard of one, but there could be. He couldn't be the only person who ever sneezed with such force. Or could he?

He put his finger under his nose. That might stop the sneezes. It always had in the past. He might have to go through the whole service as though smelling his finger. The image made him groan. Perhaps he could wear a fake mustache. That way he wouldn't need to keep his finger under his nose. Just a small mustache might work. Maybe no one would notice. After all, he was becoming a man.

Then again, he could stuff tissues into his nose. He could say he had a compound bloody nose. People would understand. Of course, if he sneezed, the tissues would become twin bullets.

For a moment, he imagined himself going against Billy the Kid. The Kid would have his hand on his holster. Danny would have his hands by his side, his head held high, and tilted way back, his nostrils pointing at the Kid. Suddenly, someone would shout "Draw" and Billy would whip his gun out of his holster — too late. "Pow! Pow!" Double barrel Kleenex bullets would fly out of Danny's nose. Faster than the speed of light, they would rip through the Kid. It would be over almost before it began.

Feeling much better, Danny reluctantly turned to his homework. He could hear his sister playing in the front yard with friends. He would rather have been outside, even if that meant playing with his sister. However, his father had threatened to take away his ticket to the upcoming professional wrestling matches if he didn't get his work done. His sister couldn't compare with that.

Danny had a science report due on camouflage in the animal kingdom. Since coming home from school — in-between attempts to make himself sneeze — he had searched the Internet for information. His desk was covered with pictures of deer, snakes, tigers, and other creatures that found ways to disguise themselves. Now, he just needed to finish his first draft.

The shouts from the front yard grew louder. Danny wrote several more paragraphs. However, his sister's voice was making it difficult to concentrate. Then he heard her scream something that made him stop writing.

"If you don't leave me alone, I'll get my brother," she yelled at someone.

Danny cringed. She wanted him to fight someone. He went to the bedroom window and looked out. Rachel was facing off with what looked to be a tall, chubby boy. Her friends had gathered behind her.

"You don't have a brother," the boy sneered.

"Danny!" Rachel yelled. She looked directly at his bedroom window.

"Danny!" the boy mimicked, nastily.

Danny hurried back to his desk. He usually didn't mind a good fight, even if it meant defending his sister. But that boy looked big. Anyway, he preferred to talk his way out of trouble. His mother said he should be a lawyer, because he was so good at talking. "He could convince you that it was the middle of the night when the sun was shining," she told neighbors, proudly.

His sister apparently preferred more direct action. "He won't just pound you," Rachel continued at full volume. "He'll sneeze on you and blow you all the way to Cleveland."

Her girlfriends laughed. Even the boy giggled. Danny turned pale.

"I'm serious," Rachel said. "His sneezes can knock down a building." She actually sounded proud. "You'd better go home before he gets here and hurts you."

The boy shrugged. "I'm not afraid of your imaginary brother," he snorted. "And I'm not afraid of a sneeze."

"You'll see!" Rachel yelled. "Da-a-a-nny!"

Danny groaned. He wasn't going to escape. He was going to be humiliated. He took a piece of paper, and tickled his nose. No sneeze. Rachel was going to demand a sneeze, and he wouldn't be able to deliver. She was always doing things like this to him. Someone would come near her, and she'd scream for help. Worse, she actually expected him to do something. She teased him all the time, called him names, tattled to their parents, but then she'd expect him to help her. It just wasn't fair.

Someone knocked on his door. "Danny?" It was Rachel's friend, Lydia. She was breathing hard from running up the stairs to his bedroom. "Rachel really needs you," she said. "I think Greg's going to hit her."

Danny stood up, slowly.

"Hurry up!" Lydia demanded, racing down the stairs.

Danny followed, emerging into the bright Ohio sunlight. Greg had cocked one hand into a fist, and was holding onto Rachel's left arm with the other.

She was wiggling, trying to get free, and yelling for help. Two other friends had backed away, obviously frightened.

Danny ran to his sister. Greg dropped Rachel's arm and turned to face him. Danny was startled to find out that he and Greg stood almost eye-to-eye. He didn't say anything for a moment, trying to calm himself. His heart was racing. Greg put his hands on his hips. That made Danny angry.

"Hi," Danny said coldly. "I'm Rachel's brother. Her big brother."

Greg's face grew hard and tense. His eyes narrowed. He clenched both fists, glaring. He looked as though he were ready to fight. Danny felt a hollow feeling in his stomach. Greg looked strong. Still, a good fight was better than homework, any day. The girls drew back. Danny made a fist, too, then pounded it into the palm of his other hand. It made a loud noise, which startled Danny almost as much as it surprised Greg.

"Danny!" Rachel cried. She ran behind him, hugging his waist. "He was going to hurt me," she whimpered.

Rachel glared at Greg. "My brother is bigger than you," she shouted.

"He's so much bigger," one of her girlfriends added, enthusiastically.

"He's stronger, too," Rachel continued.

"He's so strong," another girlfriend agreed, happily.

Danny readied his nose, aiming it toward Greg. It twitched, but didn't feel loaded for a sneeze. Any second now, he hoped. Then, Boom! He set his feet. He could imagine Greg suddenly blasted across the trees, sailing higher and higher, like a balloon losing air. Just one sneeze, he begged. But, his nose refused to respond.

The two boys simply looked at each other.

"Sneeze at him," Rachel demanded.

"I can't," Danny whispered.

"What a loser," Rachel snapped.

"He's a great loser," one of her girlfriends said.

Still talking calmly — although his heart was racing — Danny stared at Greg. "You weren't going to hit my little sister, were you?" he asked. He tried to stand as tall as he could, and, for emphasis, struck the palm of his other hand again.

Greg was obviously deciding what to do. Danny raised himself up on his tiptoes. He took deep breaths through his nose, and flexed his shoulders. He was the older of the two. Greg knew that. Sweat began to appear on Greg's forehead. His eyes looked away, then back. Danny began to smile. Greg was losing his courage.

"Were you going to hit her?" Danny repeated. He wanted to take a step forward, but Rachel's weight held him back.

Greg swallowed hard, and shook his head.

"You were going home, weren't you?" Danny continued, feeling more confident as he saw fear creep further into Greg's face.

Greg nodded. He took a step away.

"And you aren't ever going to bother her again, are you?" Danny said. He emphasized each word.

Greg shook his head.

"I hope not," Danny said. "If she tells me you bothered her, I'll ..." he paused, "I'll hit you so hard, they won't find you until they drain Lake Erie."

Greg shivered, and started running away. Once on the sidewalk, he stopped, then continued slowly down the street.

"Thank you, thank you," Rachel said, as her friends came forward to pat Danny on the arm.

"Why was he threatening you?" Danny asked.

"I think he likes me," Rachel confided. She let go of Danny.

Danny looked surprised.

"It's all in how you look at things," she explained. "I knew you wouldn't hit him. If you did, you'd hurt your hand. But Greg thinks you're a big kid. So, he's scared of you. Now, the next time I see him, he'll be nice to me.

"The problem with you," Rachel told her big brother, "is that you always think of yourself. You have to see things from someone else's point of view. This was not about you. This was about me."

"I just rescued you, and that's how you treat me?" Danny said, angrily.

"What are you going to do to me?" Rachel demanded. "Sneeze?"

"I ought to ..." Danny took a step towards her.

Rachel backed away. "If you do, I'll tell Mom," she threatened.

Danny shook his head. "You nut," he muttered under his breath, returning to his room. It would serve Greg right if Rachel became his girlfriend, Danny thought to himself. Actually, that might be more punishment than Greg deserved.

Danny sat down on his chair. Something Rachel said made him think. With a pang of regret, he realized Rachel was right. He had been looking at the world from only a very limited point of view. He thought Rachel was in trouble, and that she was being threatened by a bully. He should have seen the big picture. His little sister was manipulating him for her own ends. The problem was, he suddenly realized, that he needed a wider angle lens with which to view his role in this world.

Take his sneezing.

Sneezing wasn't something he should do to entertain his friends, or to make his Bar Mitzvah unique. No, Danny smiled. His sneezing could be put to far better use. It could be the ticket to a career in the movies or on the stage. It could be an asset, like singing or acting. His parents had always wanted him to take up an instrument. Why did he have to take one up when he could blow his own horn — his nose — without practicing.

Instead of just a Bar Mitzvah, he would give a performance. A sneeze performance. He would sneeze the "Star Spangled Banner." It was better than burping the national anthem, like his friends did. Sneezing had more class. He could go Philharmonic! Conductors would fight to lead him in the solo role of Eine Kleine Gezundtheit Musik. He might even get his own television special: "The Nose Show."

The idea delighted him. He'd be driven to opening night in a giant limousine. He'd step out into the glare of cameras. Pretty girls would beg for an autograph. He would have signature handkerchiefs to give away. "Sneeze for us," his fans would cry. But he would wait, letting the excitement build. Then, just as the tension reached its peak, he'd sneeze. Hats would go flying. Hair would be driven back. Strong men would be pinned against far walls. The girls would cry for more. Becky would be there, even though she ignored him now. And Brittany, Stephanie, and Julie, the other stuck-up girls in his Sunday School class. They would all want to talk to him, beg him to sneeze for them.

193

Danny had always wanted to be in The Guiness Book of World Records. He had hoped to enter under the category, *Bima-Stair Jumping*, but now he realized, he was limiting himself. Why jump steps when you could rattle windows? The new categories the Guiness Book would set up for him would include: Record for Loudest Sneeze, Record for Furthest Sneeze, Record for Most Devastating Sneeze, and, of course, the Record for Most Consecutive Sneezes.

There was only one major problem. He had to figure out how to sneeze on cue. And, he realized, he had to do one more thing — something so difficult, it might dissolve his dream of performing before he had a chance to begin.

In order to launch his full-time sneezing career, he had to convince his mother to let him!

There was no time to waste. Talent like his could disappear overnight. Until recently, he hadn't even known he could sneeze like this. Danny bounded down the stairs, two at a time. He always hit the stairs hard. His father usually complained that Danny sounded like a herd of buffalo, whenever he raced down the stairs. This time, Danny hit the stairs extra hard, to alert his mother. He wanted her ready to talk to him.

Mrs. Wisener was sitting in the living room, bending over a small table covered with real estate papers, when Danny arrived. He skidded around the staircase, grabbed the banister, and flung himself feet first into the living room. The table shuddered from the force of his entrance. The papers slid across the table.

"Oh, no," Mrs. Wisener yelled, throwing herself on top of the piles of papers. "I just spent an hour sorting these."

Danny looked at his mother, sprawled on top of the papers.

"I have a great idea," he announced.

Mrs. Wisener sat back, and checked the piles. They seemed in order. She wiped her forehead, and looked at Danny. "Does your idea have anything to do with apologizing for almost destroying all my hard work, or with finishing your homework?" she asked.

"No," Danny admitted.

"Then I have a better idea. You have Bar Mitzvah practice soon," Mrs. Wisener reminded him. "Finish your homework. Then we'll talk about *your* idea."

Danny scratched his head. He realized that right now might not be the best time to ask his mother for a favor, a really big favor. On the other hand, if his mother saw how important this was to him — and if he promised to memorize his Bar Mitzvah reading and be perfect at the party — maybe....

"Is Danny complaining about me?" Rachel demanded, as she rushed into the living room. She was puffing hard from running to the house, opening the heavy front door, and sprinting inside.

"About what?" Mrs. Wisener asked, curious.

Rachel glared at Danny with her hands on her hips. "You told Mom that I was teasing Greg and almost started a fight, didn't you?" she accused.

Danny started to reply, then stopped. He had a great idea. It just popped into his head. Suddenly, he realized how he could convince his mother to let him put on a sneeze show. "Listen," he said quickly. "I didn't tell Mom anything, but you thought I did, right?"

Rachel blinked.

"Rachel," Mrs. Wisener said, "what did he do?"

"Don't you see?" Danny burst out. They both looked at him. "Rachel saw me standing here, and thought I was complaining. She saw one thing, but that wasn't the real situation. Just like with Greg. I thought Rachel was mad at Greg. I didn't know she was just teasing him."

"You were mad at Greg?" Mrs. Wisener asked Rachel. "Who's Greg?"

"Who?" Rachel asked, innocently. She looked

196

angrily at Danny again, turned, and quickly went back outside.

Mrs. Wisener watched her for a moment, then looked at Danny. "What are you talking about?" she asked.

"My Bar Mitzvah party," Danny told her. "You see, I've been looking at things the wrong way. Like your papers here. I just see piles of paper. I don't like them because I want to talk to you, and you need to work with them."

"But, Danny," Mrs. Wisener said. "These are very important papers. I use them to sell homes. That makes us a lot of money, and helps pay for your clothes, your skates, your baseball glove, and many other things."

"That's my point," Danny shouted excitedly. "See? It's the same papers on the table, but we're looking at them from different points of view."

Mrs. Wisener started to say something, then stopped. Danny watched her carefully. His mother seemed to be thinking. "What about your Bar Mitz-vah party?" she asked thoughtfully.

"Yes," he said excitedly. "I was wondering about it. You know, I'm sneezing ...."

His mother had a serious look on her face.

"You're worried about your sneezing spoiling the ceremony, aren't you?" Mrs. Wisener asked, not giving him a chance to answer her. "I had no idea you

197

were so thoughtful. I was just thinking about how much money we were spending to make a good impression. But you were thinking about the true meaning of a Bar Mitzvah."

"I was?" Danny managed.

His mother hugged him. "I'm very proud of you," she said. "I need to change my point of view, too. You really are becoming a man. I need to talk to the Rabbi. He must think I'm awful after what I said about your Bar Mitzvah. It's not about a party, is it?" She patted Danny's shoulder. "But you knew that, didn't you?"

"I did?" Danny said, hesitantly.

"I'm going to take you to the Synagogue. It's time for your rehearsal with the Cantor," Mrs. Wisener said.

She started up the stairs, then came back down and hugged him again. There were tears in her eyes. "I wish my father were here to see you. He used to *daven* every day, and helped train the young boys for their Bar Mitzvah. Maybe," she said, "you'll follow in his footsteps."

She went upstairs, then stopped again and looked back at him. "We've been so caught up in modern life, we've forgotten the real value of Judaism. Your father will be very proud of you."

Danny watch her disappear. "But what about my career?" he called after her.

Danny didn't sneeze through his entire practice with Cantor Roseland. He kept expecting to. He sniffed once or twice in preparation, but his nose did not react. He thought about warning the Cantor about the power of his sneezing, but wasn't sure how to explain that one moment the Cantor might be chanting the Torah portion, and the next he might be flying across the room.

From the doorway, Danny could see that his mother had gone to the Rabbi's office. He wondered what they were talking about. He knew they weren't going to be discussing his sneezing ability, or how that ability could be used to brighten up his party and launch his entertainment career.

Cantor Roseland continued to correct his singing. Once or twice he distorted his face, reminding Danny of how his classmates looked when the science teacher scraped the blackboard with chalk, in order to get their attention. Danny's singing sounded fine to his own ears, but the Cantor always looked like he was in such pain. Danny figured that at the Cantor's age, he couldn't hear that well any more, and so, Danny sang as loud as possible. With Danny, loud meant high, and his voice seemed to vibrate the Cantor's glasses.

"Time to go," Cantor Roseland announced. "Now, remember to think quiet thoughts. You don't have to shout. And don't get sick," he cautioned, as Danny ran out.

Danny hurried to the Rabbi's office. He stopped by the door and saw his mother in a chair. Only the top of the Rabbi's balding head was visible.

"Come in," Rabbi Gordon said. "We were just talking about you. What a *mensch* you are."

Mrs. Wisener patted the chair next to her. Danny entered, but decided to stand. "I told him what you said," she told her son.

Danny shuddered silently. Did the Rabbi already know about his sneezing plans? He would be harder to convince. The Rabbi was very practical, and was always looking for kids to accomplish things.

Well, he could accomplish a good sneeze.

The Rabbi's entire office was covered with books, newspapers, magazines, and papers. Nothing was placed in piles. The room looked as though someone had simply scattered everything, filling all the empty space on his desk and on most of the floor, with paper.

Danny thought that one really good sneeze and there would be a tremendous paper snowstorm. That would be an accomplishment even the Rabbi would take note of. Danny tried to create a sneeze, but couldn't.

"Ah, ah, ah," he tried.

"Oh! Oh! Okay," his mother sounded the alarm, grabbing onto the arms of her chair. Rabbi Gordon slammed his arms on top of the closest stack of papers.

"Sorry," Danny said. "False alarm."

Rabbi Gordon managed a smile. He nervously patted the papers, as if assuring them.

"I may even give a sermon on your idea," Rabbi Gordon said. "Right now, I'm preparing material for my religion class at Akron University. I thought I would talk about the Holocaust. There are still many people who insist it never happened," the Rabbi said. "The evidence is all there. The pictures. The testimony. I don't know why people can't see it."

Mrs. Wisener agreed. "The truth is, people don't always want to see what's really the truth.

"Danny has helped me to look at things very differently," Mrs. Wisener continued. "I know lots of children believe a Bar Mitzvah marks the end of their Jewish studies. Danny has shown me that's not true. It can be the beginning, too."

Mrs. Wisener looked at her son. "Danny, you are going to learn so much more in the coming years. The Rabbi and I have been talking. Thanks to your enthusiasm, he plans to set up a whole new series of classes for young boys and girls after their Bar or Bat Mitzvah."

"The party—?" Danny tried to explain how he felt. Somehow, he had convinced his mother of the wrong thing. He didn't want more classes. He wanted more sneezes. His mother was a businesswoman. Didn't she realize his special ability was an incredible opportunity? There couldn't be anyone else with his talent. He could probably jump stairs and sneeze at the same time, setting a double record.

"Danny," the Rabbi said. "I now realize you are much more serious than I thought, and that you believe a party might be frivolous. But really, a party is all right. You should enjoy your accomplishment, and share it with your friends and relatives."

Danny decided not to say anything. Without meaning to, he had almost obliterated his party. One more word and he might find himself — on the day of his party — studying Bible with the Rabbi. Worse yet, practicing with Cantor Roseland to join the Synagogue choir.

Rabbi Gordon sat back. "That's some idea you had," he said, approvingly.

"It was Rachel's," Danny burst out.

"Isn't that just like him," Mrs. Wisener said. "Sharing the credit with his little sister. I've so misjudged him."

Danny shrugged. "I hate to give her credit," he

202

admitted. "She's pretty obnoxious."

"From one perspective," Rabbi Gordon corrected.

"No, that's pretty unanimous, if you don't count Greg," Danny insisted.

"But she's just nine years old," Rabbi Gordon said. He caught himself. "There I go again, looking at something from just one viewpoint."

The Rabbi began to rummage through a stack of books on his desk. Several plummeted to the floor and landed with a soft plop. "Now, where's my speech?" asked the Rabbi. He began pushing and prodding all the papers. A few teetered dangerously but stayed upright. "I wanted to share it with you, before I read it to the congregation," he announced.

"Don't worry if you can't find it," Danny told him. "I'll probably sneeze in the middle of your speech and send the congregation on a trip around the world," Danny said, hopefully.

Rabbi Gordon smiled. "I don't think sneezing is going to be a problem anymore. We have a lot of allergists who belong to the Temple. I talked to some of them. I think we've figured out what's causing your sneezes. Come, let's go into the sanctuary, and I'll show you."

The Rabbi led the way into the sanctuary. The large room was dark, with just the eternal light flickering above the great doors of the Ark. The eternal light hung from a long chain attached to the high ceiling, but in the dark it looked like it was suspended in air.

Danny walked slowly toward the bima. Everything seemed so different. On Shabbat, he would walk in, feeling comfortable because everything was so familiar. Now, the sanctuary was strange, and yet enticing. He felt a sense of awe and wonder.

Rabbi Gordon reached the front of the Ark, and opened the doors. Danny stopped by the steps. Just a few days ago, he had set a world record with a single leap. But right now, he wasn't interested in world records.

As the Ark doors opened wide, Danny waited for his nose to react. It remained silent. He didn't even feel a tingle.

The lights from inside the Ark flooded the bima. The Torahs never looked more beautiful. They were nestled in their holders with white coverings trimmed with gold. The silver crowns on top of the wooden staves caught the light, and reflected it even more brightly, creating a shimmering image that thrilled him.

The Rabbi took an ornament from the closest Torah. He waved Danny closer. Danny stepped onto the bima. Rabbi Gordon held out the gleaming ornament towards him. Almost instantly, Danny felt his eyes start to fill with water. His nose tensed, like a cannon about to be fired.

"Ah, ah..." he cried, and backed away. But it was too late.

"...chooo," Danny finished. The blast started the eternal light swaying. It rattled the great doors of the Ark, and sent papers on the podium flying through the air.

The Rabbi replaced the ornament and closed the Ark.

Dazed and unhappy, Danny plopped down on the closest chair, and tried to clear his head. How would he be able to recite his Bar Mitzvah reading? No one in the first five rows would be safe. He was sure they would have to erect a glass partition between him and the congregation.

Would they begin handing out umbrellas when he got up on the bima, or post a sign: "Caution: Sitting within 20 feet of the Bar Mitzvah boy can be hazardous to your health?"

If he only knew why he sneezed on the bima, and not anywhere else.

Still, Danny thought, the idea of blasting his sister in Synagogue did have promise. He would be reading calmly, and kapow! She'd get it right between the eyes. As everyone said, "*Gezundtheit*," Rachel would be orbiting. He'd apologize, and continue reading. And what could she do? Complain? In the middle of a service?

Rabbi Gordon sat next to him. He rumpled Danny's hair. "You're probably wondering why you sneeze in here, aren't you?"

"I wish I knew the secret," he said.

"I can understand why you're upset," the Rabbi continued. "You want to stop, but can't."

A sly smile worked its way along the Rabbi's lips.

"Danny, I've got good news for you. The Temple custodian recently polished the Torah ornaments with a special kind of cleanser. There's a warning on the label that says that some people have an allergy to some of the chemicals. You must be one of those people," the Rabbi explained. "We all thought you were allergic to the Torah, but the truth is, no one is allergic to the Torah."

The Synagogue was very quiet as Rabbi Gordon approached the Ark. Danny's father and mother stood across from him. They were both nervous. Danny wasn't. He turned, so he could look inside the Ark when it opened. As always, he felt a surge of excitement as the Rabbi pulled on the doors.

The secret interior of the Ark appeared with its gleaming white surface, and its three precious scrolls.

The Rabbi reached in and took out the middle Torah. He placed it on his shoulder and stepped back.

This Torah scroll did not glisten with any silver ornaments. It had a simple, white covering with no gold braid. Its handles were bare wood without any polish on them. Indeed, for the first time since they had been set into the Ark, none of the Torahs had the slightest bit of adornment.

There was a quiet stirring in the congregation as people recognized the ornaments were missing. Some whispered that there may have been a robbery.

Of course, people were missing the big picture.

This wasn't about the Torah ornaments. It was about Danny. It was about sneezing. It was also about reading his Bar Mitzvah portion, which he did, almost without mistakes.

And, of course, it was about growing up. Danny realized that depending on your nose for your future, instead of your head and your heart, left you with nowhere to go.

As the end of the service reached its climax, Rabbi Gordon held up the Torah and showed it to the congregation. "This is the oldest document still in daily use anywhere in the world," he announced. "It doesn't need any decorations to proclaim its importance, and its value. It is a symbol to all of us. We Jews have always looked at the Torah from the inside, and not from the outside. It's how we look at the world."

He smiled at Danny. "Danny, I want you to follow in the ways of the Torah as you enter this important stage of your life. There are many messages in your Torah reading that can help mold you, and help you find your way in this world. They are Torah messages handed down through the generations.

"Danny," the Rabbi concluded, "I know I don't have to tell you — they are nothing to sneeze at."